MIDLIFE WOMEN

LR/LEND/001

The Jones and Bartlett Series in Nursing

MIDLIFE WOMEN
CONTEMPORARY ISSUES

Joan Mathews Jacobson, Ph.D., R.N.

Department of Nursing
Simmons College
Boston, Massachusetts

Jones and Bartlett Publishers

Boston   London

Editorial, Sales, and Customer Service Offices

Jones and Bartlett Publishers
One Exeter Plaza
Boston, MA 02116
617-859-3900
800-832-0034

Jones and Bartlett Publishers International
7 Melrose Terrace
London W6 7RL
England

Library of Congress Cataloging-in-Publication Data
Jacobson, Joan Mathews.
  Midlife women : contemporary issues / Joan Mathews Jacobson.
    p.   cm.
  Includes bibliographical references and index.
  ISBN 0-86720-929-1
  1. Middle aged women.   2. Middle aged women—Health and hygiene.
I. Title.
HQ1059.4.J35   1995
305.4—dc20   94–42098
                                                              CIP

Acquisitions Editor: Jan Wall
Production Editor: Nadine Fitzwilliam
Manufacturing Buyer: Dana L. Cerrito
Typesetting: Ultra Graphics
Cover Design: Beth Santos
Printing and Binding: Braun-Brumfield, Inc.
Cover Printing: New England Book Components, Inc.

Printed in the United States of America
99 98 97 96 95   10 9 8 7 6 5 4 3 2 1

Contents

Preface

I wrote this book with two distinct groups of midlife women in mind. Initially, I intended it for the academic study of midlife women set in a comprehensive framework. I wanted to address issues other than the menopause surrounding the midlife transition in women. I felt it was important to report not only the biological issues, but also the history and theoretical background in which women are viewed. I also wanted to share my own research findings that validate that the midlife experience for most women is different from the mainly negative portrayal found in the literature. I envisioned that this book would serve as an adjunct text for graduate and undergraduate courses in women's health, and women in general.

However, as I shared the project with friends and colleagues it became more apparent that there is widespread interest among the general population of midlife women for such a book. These women express a need for information that is unbiased and generally unavailable. They are looking for an overview of how we got to where we are, and what to expect during this dynamic and exciting life transition. And so, it is my hope that women who are not pursuing academic studies at this time in their lives will also find this a useful guide.

Acknowledgments

When I think of any project or creative achievement that one completes in a lifetime, I am reminded of a story told by Norman Augustine, the Chairman of the Board of the Martin Marrietta Corporation upon receiving an award from the National Academy of Engineering. He said, "Remember the next time you see a frog sitting on top of a flag pole, he didn't get there alone."

I remember the countless individuals who placed their faith in me and projected me along. I hope that all of you midlife women who participated in my research, as well as other midlife colleagues and friends who encouraged me in my work will accept my gratitude.

Penny Richardson, my graduate school advisor and mentor at the University of Southern California, was my greatest fan. She believed I could succeed through the rigors of the PhD program and I did. She would have enjoyed reading this book. I miss her so, as do all of her many admirers. She left this world in 1993.

David Peterson, Director of the Leonard Davis School of Gerontology at the University of Southern California, was another mentor who helped me gain the knowledge I needed to reach my vision.

Lois Banner of the Center for the Study of Women and Men in Society was another force who opened my eyes. Her scholarly work and provocative books about the experience of women were a driving force and inspiration long after I left the University of Southern California.

There are numerous others who were always there to encourage, listen, and even write letters on my behalf. Among these are Lew and Barbara Allen, and Bertha and David Bradburn, who helped calculate my data on the ferry to Nantucket. Cleo and Bob Moss, and Jerry Slatter, what friends they are!

Old graduate school friends, Doctors Susan and Jess Carreon, read through the raw manuscript and shared their insights. It was an honor to be read by Susan, an Administrative Dean at Golden West College, and Jess, President of Ventura College in California.

Thanks to my dear neighbor, Thania Rios, for always listening and offering sage advice.

An accomplished new friend, Nancy Sobel, MD, PhD, was very kind and rigorous in her review of the chapter on health and psychological issues. As an expert gynecologist, pharmacologist, and Lahey Clinic associate, Nancy has added credibility to my convictions. Anne Branscomb inspired me to continue through her many accomplishments and, vicariously, through her newly published book on the information explosion and its impact on all of our lives. I would also like to thank Debbie Allinger, PhD, who became not only my statistical analyst, but also my friend.

My editor, Jan Wall, who believed we had something to say about midlife and the baby-boom generation, has been a strong and unswerving support. I remember fondly another editor, Sheila Gibbons, now Director of Public Affairs for the Gannett Corporation (USA and a host of other newspapers). She gave me my first chance at this with the "Ask Joan" column in *LadyCom* Magazine.

My children Betsy and Brian Klene; Matt Jacobson, who used to find books for me to read on midlife women when he was in high school; and Jim and Mary Jacobson have all wondered at times what their mother was about; thanks for listening and understanding. Someday this may be of interest to my adorable granddaughters Brigitte and Jane Klene; grandsons Charlie Klene, and Will, Patrick, and Colin Jacobson.

Finally, my dear Jake. Thanks for bearing with me, for reading the manuscript, for your unending technical advice and computer knowledge, your moral support, and most of all your love. This one's for you.

Introduction

Many women approach growing older and the appearance of the first wrinkles with fear and trepidation because they know so little about what to expect in the middle years. Most researchers identify around age 35 as the beginning of middle age, a time when we begin to confront our own mortality. However, this is an arbitrary designation that may change in the future as roles and societal expectations change. For the purposes of this book and with the consensus from various sources, midlife begins between ages 35 and 40 up to age 65. Neugarten (1968) sets the launching of children, reaching a peak in one's occupation, menopause, grandparenthood, retirement, onset of chronic illness, and widowhood as the midlife parameters. The middle years may be classified, re-named, and lengthened by future researchers in light of changing societal norms caused by the baby-boom generation and increasing productive longevity.

Many 35-year-old women are surprised when they learn that they have been designated as middle-aged. This was the average age when older midlife women who worked at home sent their youngest children off to school. Furthermore, it was often the period when their elder parents began to demand attention. Some women entering midlife may feel unfulfilled at the prospect of not having experienced marriage or motherhood. Other midlife women have been in the work force during marriage and child-rearing. For working women, the transition into midlife may be less painful, but midlife presents many unknowns having to deal with the physical and social changes in aging. Midlife is a relatively new phenomena because of increasing longevity and generally fewer debilitating diseases. During the early years of this century, reaching middle age was rare, as few individuals lived past their mid-40s. The relatively few identified norms for midlife development are changing radically.

Those who have chosen to marry and bear children present an entirely different lifestyle than those who have not married or borne children. Some of the older cohorts of midlife women are reminded of the passage of time as their children mature and begin to make their own way in the world. As the family becomes less dependent on the mother as caretaker, she must find new interests to occupy her time. In most instances, having children grow up and leave home is greeted with pleasure in anticipation of new freedoms. However, many women do not foresee the growing pains that may accompany this freedom. Much has been said, but little written, about this particular stage in every woman's life, and it is becoming increasingly difficult to separate myth from reality. This is especially true when one adds the dimension of the initial members of the baby-boom generation, born following World War II, who are now in their fourth decade, and recently entering the ranks of their older counterparts in midlife. These women were raised differently from those women now in midlife who preceded them. Both the younger and older midlife cohorts display intense curiosity about whether the changes in society have made them different from those women who came before.

A lack of empirical study on women in this stage of life has perpetuated societal myths regarding midlife women. Earlier studies laid the groundwork for modern theory and myth about the middle years. These studies reflected mainly on the work that Sigmund Freud performed during the nineteenth century about life in Austria. Freud focused solely on female patients who were emotionally disturbed and attributed their characteristics to all women. Other studies, from which much of the present theory about midlife is derived, were based primarily on male subjects and conducted by male researchers. As a result, when women were studied, using the same criteria as those created for the studies on male subjects, they were considered deviant if they did not conform to the male model for midlife. It is only recently that researchers are discovering how different the developmental processes are for each of the sexes. Contemporary societal changes and the advent of the baby-boom generation have caused the slow erosion of many misconceptions and myths about midlife. Preconceived notions and myths are slow to change, even in the face of an emerging body of research performed with women as the investigators.

I first became interested in midlife when I was in my mid-30s and my own life began to change drastically. At the time, my three children aged 11, 14, and 17 were growing up. Suddenly, I had more time on my hands and began to think about what I was going to do for the rest of my life. I made a plan to return to school and, eventually, to the work force. I told myself, "I am in my mid-30s and I probably have at least 40 more years to be productive after the children leave home." I wanted to be in a position to make a meaningful contribution following child-rearing. Almost simultaneously, I began reading Gail Sheehy's *Passages* (1976), mainly a compilation of others' work, and found its apt descriptions of universal experiences occurring in many midlife individuals very helpful. After staying out of the work force for 10 years while I cared for my three children, I found myself working part time and returning to school for a graduate degree. So many changes were occurring in my life that I felt impelled to study other women of my age. I wanted to know if they were having the same feelings as I, and how they were coping.

It is well recognized that midlife is a very significant stage in the life cycle; during this transition foundations are laid for later life. Many women in the older cohort, in their late 50s and early 60s, spent their early adult years nurturing and caring for their families. These women came of age during an entirely different set of circumstances than the women of the baby-boom generation. Some of them experienced the Great Depression and World War II and were, for the most part, raised with the traditional values of home and family. It was rare for those in the older cohort of midlife women to have worked for wages outside the home. This was prevalent only if they were poor or were among the few women in the professions during those times. These older midlife women experienced fewer opportunities in education and they had limited access to male-dominated professions such as medicine, law, and business. Theirs was a period in which patriotism and national consensus flourished. As their children grew up and left home, these women were faced with the dilemma of how to redefine their lives.

Historically, it was during this time that many older midlife women began returning to school, work, or became involved in volunteer activities. Most older midlife women, born during the late 1920s and 1930s, made the transition with ease, but for those few who had difficulty dealing with new roles anxiety, stress, and depression were often the by-product (Rubin, 1979; McKinlay & McKinlay, 1986; Jacobson, 1993). Some older midlife women have been rendered incapable of adequately supporting themselves without drastic changes in lifestyle following, increasingly common, midlife divorce. There has been little in the way of societal support for older midlife women as illustrated by the effects of no-fault divorce, inequitable community property settlements, and diminishing alimony payments. Often, society sends mixed messages to women in the process of child-rearing, as single mothers, or functioning as older divorced women.

In addition, any frank discussion about the physical changes that occur around age 45 to 55 has been suppressed by societal norms as something that we just don't talk about. This phase in women's lives has been treated both as an illness and a mysterious ailment. Very little information is available to pre-menopausal women about "the change" or what to expect during the menopause. Information that has been forthcoming has usually been transmitted by word-of-mouth between family and friends. The medical profession has traditionally offered very little support for symptoms of menopause, such as hot flashes, other than tranquilizers and hormones. The older generation of midlife women were not socialized to question the treatment offered by often paternalistic and ill-informed physicians. These physicians treated menopause as an illness. Slowly, the medical community has been influenced, in some instances by new technology, to be more receptive in using alternative treatment. More recently, the younger cohort of midlife women, consumers of their own care, have questioned some of the rather invasive and drastic treatments previously offered to women in the menopause.

The baby-boom women, born following January 1, 1946, have only recently entered the middle years. They have been portrayed as more liberal and less conforming than women born a generation earlier. Baby-boom women had more career and educational opportunities, later marriage, and more sexual freedom than those who preceded them. Some in the baby-boom cohort were among the first to experience the benefits of equal opportunity for women that came about as a result of the feminist and civil rights movements. For the most part, the baby boomers came of age during an era of affluence, television, sexual revolution, proliferation of illegal drug use, and Vietnam protests against government. Patriotism as it was formerly known appeared to cease being a mainstream American value.

Within this book, I focus on the unique issues faced by baby-boom women in midlife by presenting a perspective on what transpired in the past and what the future may bring. The major task before us is to examine how societal changes have affected the life satisfaction and health of the newest members of the midlife cohort, the baby boomers. The discussion in Chapter 1 presents a contemporary perspective of women in history and an explanation of feminist issues. In Chapter 2 some of the existing and relevant theories about this most pivotal of the life stages are described. In Chapter 3 some of the pressing health and psychological issues that have been expressed by midlife women will be explored. Chapter 4 is a discussion of my own research concerning the experiences and differences between a representative group of college-educated baby-boom women and their older counterparts in midlife. The final chapter contains a discussion on the implications for the future with coping strategies for successful aging. What happens in this important transition will be predictive of the later years.

Not much has changed in how midlife women are perceived. There is a dramatic explosion in the numbers of contemporary women between the ages of 35 and 65. Increasingly, women are realizing that they must be advocates of their own destinies by becoming educated, well-informed, and by demanding answers. One can only hope this exploration of women's experiences will inspire us to deeper insights on how we abide our midlives in an ever-changing world now and into the twenty-first century.

References

Jacobson, J.M. (1995). *Risk factors for breast cancer. Preliminary findings.* Unpublished.

McKinlay J. & McKinlay S. (1986). *Women and their health in Massachusetts.* Cambridge, MA: Cambridge Research Center.

Neugarten, B. (1968). *Middle age and aging.* Chicago: University of Chicago Press.

Rubin, L. (1979). *Women of a certain age.* New York: Harper & Row.

Sheehy, G. (1976). *Passages.* New York: Bantam Books.

Chapter 1

History and Contemporary Women's Experience

Looking Back

The experience of women from an historical perspective gives us much needed insight into present roles and dilemmas facing midlife women, especially those in the baby-boom generation. Unless they have been educated with a feminist perspective, most women in the baby-boom generation have little knowledge of the experience of women in past generations. They are not cognizant of the struggle that has yielded increasing freedom and acceptance of the place of women in society. As a result, any misconceptions about this most important passage abound. The middle years are often mistakenly associated solely with the menopause experience, with little reference to the myriad of other important issues. Most women have an uneventful menopause (McKinlay & McKinlay, 1986), but other eventful contemporary midlife experiences are often dwarfed by comparison. Some of these events are described as divorce, remarriage, stepparenting, re-entry into the work force or school, launching children, or in the case of some women, childbearing and child-rearing.

To avoid a future fraught with misunderstandings and misconceptions, it would be wise to look into events previously experienced by women. Studying the past may present a model and a direction for the future. An historical approach will show how cultural attitudes have influenced women's perceptions over time.

It is interesting to note that relatively few models of midlife development have evolved. This may be explained by the fact that in the past most individuals did not experience midlife. It is only recently, with the development of advanced medical technology and antibiotics, that the life expectancy has increased to 78.3 years for women and 71.3 for men (National Center for Health Statistics, 1990). At the turn of the century average life expectancy was only 47 years. The fact that men do not live as long as women is also a cause for concern in our society, the implication being that many women will outlive their male counterparts, marriage partners, and "significant others" and spend their final years alone. Frequently, this occurs simultaneously with diminished resources and ill health. How the tasks of the middle years are managed will be predictive of the way old age is experienced by the women in the baby-boom generation.

In my teaching experience, many students have been incredulous to learn that women in the United States have only been "allowed to be educated" at the college or university level since 1837. Add to this the fact that women have only been given the right to vote for the President of the United States since 1924 (Horowitz-Lefkowitz, 1984).

It is also true that few women have been chronicled in the history books. See how many you can name. How about Joan of Arc, Catherine the Great, Madame Curie, Florence Nightingale, Eleanor Roosevelt, and how many others? Most women in the past have been relegated to the private sphere of domesticity. Often, they lived lives of dependency and inferiority, and were given little recognition for their contributions to society.

In *The Feminist Papers*, Rossi (1973) reviewed over a thousand documents covering a one hundred-year span between 1770 and 1870. Memoirs, biographies, and other documents were explored from a feminist perspective in order to piece together some of the mysteries surrounding women's lives, and possibly to revise history. The account of personal lives of women, both contented and discontented, revealed the origins of feminist expression.

Early English Feminism

Rossi describes the life of an English woman, Mary Wollstonecraft, born in 1759. Mary was among the first women in recorded history to have lived with her lover, whom she later married, out of wedlock. A free spirit, she left an unhappy home life to wander about the country and seek her fortune. She supported herself by engaging in numerous ventures and eventually by writing several books and essays including *Thoughts on the Education of Daughters*, a biography entitled *Mary*, and a children's book entitled *Original Stories*. However, she is most noted for her landmark work *A Vindication of the Rights of Women*. Her writings were influenced by both the American and French Revolutions, which, in turn, led to a campaign for the equal rights for women. She deplored the fact that girls were not thought bright enough to be educated, and demanded that the British government provide public education for the female gender. It was her premise that women's talents were being wasted, and that the only way they could gain social status was through marriage. She argued that women would be better wives and mothers and would take better care of themselves if they were educated, and treated with equality.

Wollstonecraft is revered as being the inspiration for later feminist ideals and for promoting equal rights for women. She is credited with raising the consciousness of men in England and, subsequently, influencing the course of history. It has been only recently that Wollstonecraft's accomplishments have been recognized, mainly through Rossi's efforts.

Colonial America

Horowitz-Lefkowitz (1984) wrote about the plight of women in colonial America. They were expected to share in chores and participate in establishing the household because there were so few workers available. However, there was a strict division of labor with the women working in the private/home sphere, while men were responsible for obligations outside the home. Early American women were taught to read and write so that they might read the Bible. Women were responsible for teaching their children to share in the religious life of the community. Girls, most often educated at home, were instructed to be pure, submissive, and pious. When formal education was established, only boys received a classical education in Greek, Latin, philosophy, and history to prepare them for college.

Harvard was founded in 1636, but only young men were permitted to attend. Girls were eventually admitted to public education at this time, but continued to receive different preparation than boys.

In most colonial towns and provinces, except for Rhode Island, colonial women could neither inherit nor own property, nor could they vote or be considered equal members of society. Banner (1984) noted similar restrictions as late as the late nineteenth century. She reported that until the latter part of the twentieth century, women in many areas of the United States were forbidden by archaic laws to enter into business contracts without their husband's permission. It was only recently that, in many states, women still were not allowed to apply for a credit card without a husband's authorization.

Post-Revolutionary America

Abigail Adams is remembered for entreating her husband, John, the president of the United States, "to remember the ladies" when he was helping to draft the Constitution of the United States (Rossi, 1973). But it was not until the passage of the nineteenth amendment, in 1920, that women were finally given the right to vote. Women have been seeking equality ever since, and many are still seeking these rights.

The Nineteenth Century

The industrial revolution during the late 1800s caused many changes in the lives of women. Young working-class women were sought after, and subsequently exploited in order to enhance the work force. In Lowell, Massachusetts, the textile industry employed young women and paid them half of what men earned for the same jobs. The rationale for this was that women were not expected to support a family with their wages. The "Ladies of Lowell," as they were called, were expected to work 12 to 14 hours a day, six days a week. They were housed in company-run rooming houses, complete with housemothers, where they remained for an average of five years. Many of these women worked to contribute to their families' welfare, while they toiled to put a brother through college, or to earn their dowries (Kessler-Harris, 1982). Although this was an era in which women were exploited, it was the first time in our history that it became acceptable to venture out of the agrarian social system and into the public sphere. Many of these young women may have actually felt liberated rather than exploited. However, when they returned home or married they re-entered the sphere of domesticity.

Education and Employment

By the end of the nineteenth century, educational opportunities in women's colleges were plentiful. Over 11,000 women were now enrolled in colleges across the country. Mount Holyoke, founded in 1837, was the first women's college. It was followed by Vassar in 1865, Wellesley and Smith, both in Massachusetts, by 1875, Bryn Mawr in 1885, Barnard, an annex of Columbia College, in 1889, and Radcliffe in 1893. These colleges comprise "the seven sisters" schools (Horowitz-Lefkowitz, 1984). It is astonishing that over 200 years were to elapse after the founding of Harvard before women in America would be allowed the benefits of secondary education. The formation of these colleges marked the beginning of advanced education for women.

According to Banner (1984), women's colleges were established because men's colleges refused to admit women. Other colleges, such as the land-grant state colleges, became coed because of the shortage of students. Slowly, a very few women were permitted to enter law and medical schools. However, most college women at the turn of the century were educated to become teachers or missionaries.

During this time, only 5% of all women worked outside the home. In addition to those working as teachers and missionaries, the few women who did work outside the home were employed as clerks, factory workers, doctors, nurses, lawyers, and actresses. Some women worked in their homes taking in boarders or participating in cottage industry production. Often, this was the only means of support for the many widowed or abandoned nineteenth century women.

Sexuality

Nineteenth-century societal mores demanded the Victorian code consisting of overt suppression of sexuality. There was virtually no sex education and young women entered marriage with little or no knowledge of their sexuality. The American ideal was the Gibson Girl who was portrayed as young, beautiful, and rebellious. This ideal is noted by Banner (1984) as one of the key influences at the root of the movement for more freedom for women.

Contrary to the outward Victorian attitude, there was an expanding undercurrent of prostitution. For some, prostitution was a means of support. Many of these women freely engaged in their trade, enjoying sexual freedom and rebelling against the establishment. It is also thought that working-class women engaged in uninhibited sexual activity (Banner, 1984). These behaviors might be explained as a reaction to the mainstream, narrow-minded, and sexually restrictive Victorian lifestyle. Women in this era were expected to conform to the prevailing social norms and were denied the chance to achieve their full potential. In any event, Banner (1984) reported that women in the working classes were not as sexually inhibited as those in the upper classes.

Very little is known about women who were poor, black, or from non-mainstream ethnic backgrounds. It is known that they worked in menial jobs and were underpaid and undereducated. They were denied admission when the women's colleges were first established. Sadly, most schools of higher education were slow to admit minority and lower-class women before the civil rights and women's movements in the 1960s and 1970s (Banner, 1984).

Childbirth

Childbirth during this era was treated as an illness in the upper classes. On the other hand, working-class women were far from being pampered, and were expected to return to work within days of delivery. "The Family and Medical Leave Act," granting twelve weeks of maternity leave to all employed women, was not passed by the Congress of the United States until 1993. Since 57% of the work force is made up of women, this is a major breakthrough in recognizing the multiple roles of women in both the workplace and society (Swasy, July 23, 1993).

It is also important to note that there was a declining birthrate around the turn of the century. This deliberate action may imply that women were choosing to take charge of their own bodies. Limited availability of modern techniques and antibiotics caused many women to lose their lives during childbirth. This may have also contributed to the declining birthrate.

Simultaneously with the decline in fertility, the doors of higher education were finally opening to women. Choosing singlehood was another option that was becoming acceptable as more women became well educated. Many chose to pursue careers and forego submission to a restricted, and often life-threatening, lifestyle. Many college educated women were, for the first time in history, rejecting the rigors of Victorian marriage and childbearing (Banner, 1983).

The Suffragette Movement

Other trends in women's history were becoming obvious as the suffragette movement proliferated. Many in society at this time discounted these libertarian women, but the loud voice in support of women's equality was not to be denied. Through the efforts of Elizabeth Cady Stanton and Susan B. Anthony, renowned activists in the suffragette movement, a more relaxed dress code was adopted. Through their efforts, hoop skirts and corsets were finally discarded. They noted that hoop skirts, corsets, and stays were actually dangerous to women's health and safety. Hoop skirts were especially targeted because their bulkiness made it difficult for women to move about easily, much less flee from a burning building, or participate in sports. Thus, relaxed dress styles allowed women to become active in sports and other outside activities (Banner, 1983).

The Twentieth Century

The Early Years

America was still maturing in the early twentieth century when our country was brought out of complacency by the first world war. Fortunately, our participation in the war was limited and it ended in 1918, followed by a new era of prosperity and freedom.

During the post-war years, technology applied to the use of electricity brought about inventions such as the washing machine, the refrigerator, the electric iron, and the toaster. These inventions allowed middle-class women to have more time for leisure and volunteer activities.

Many families abandoned their farms and the agrarian lifestyle and migrated to the cities. During the early 1920s, a carefree lifestyle and a new fashion in clothing was portrayed by the flappers. They wore scandalously short skirts and loose dresses and were perceived as sexually free and appealing. Short, loose clothing, and, for the more adventurous, bathing suits, became the vogue during the Roaring Twenties in the United States (Banner, 1983).

Working-class women had a different experience. They found themselves in the ranks with many new immigrants, widows, and unmarried daughters. They worked long hours in factories, many in the newly emerging garment industry, and anywhere else that they could make a living (Banner, 1984).

The massive immigration from Europe during the late nineteenth and early twentieth centuries had a huge influence on the fate of American women. Immigrants from Ireland, Italy, Spain, and other European countries settled in large urban areas like New York and Boston. Their immense numbers taxed the resources of the cities, forcing reform in both health care and sanitation practices.

Notable women such as Lillian Wald and Jane Adams formed settlement houses in the lower east side of New York City. They provided home health care predominantly to poor women and children. Their efforts eventually led to the development of Visiting Nurses Associations that have proliferated throughout the nation. These pioneers in women's health organized the early health departments and influenced how health was to be maintained, and communicable disease prevented.

Soon after the settlement houses were established, Margaret Sanger and Charlotte Perkins Gillman instigated the birth control movement (Banner, 1984). This served to assist women in managing their own destinies by planning the number of children that they wanted to have. Women were finally becoming recognized as having some influence within the social system. The control that women had over their own bodies was firmly instituted. Despite these earlier efforts, control over fertility is still an issue in the 1990s in spite of legislation giving women the right to abortion.

Twenty-four percent of all women participated in the work force by the late 1920s and early 1930s. In spite of increased visibility in the public sector, women were still being paid lower wages than men for the same jobs. As a result of this exploitation and other forces, such as 14-hour work days, the labor union movement emerged (Banner, 1984).

Women were at last making lives for themselves outside of the domestic setting. Amelia Earhart was acclaimed as the first woman to fly an airplane. As airplane travel proliferated, women were accepted into the emerging industry as air hostesses or "stewardesses" as they were first called, but not as pilots. In addition to requirements such as correct weight and pleasing personalities, air hostesses were also required to be qualified as registered nurses. The primary role for these women was to serve as assistants to male pilots and their passengers (Hochschild, 1983). However, air hostesses were perceived and envied by many as having exciting and glamorous existences especially by women who were relegated to the sphere of domesticity.

There is no doubt that the seeds of unrest cast in the late nineteenth and early twentieth centuries by the suffragette movement resulted in the explosion of the women's rights movement during the turbulent 1960s. This earlier movement culminated with the passage of the nineteenth amendment in 1920. Women participated, for the first time, in the presidential elections in 1924.

It was thought by many women that once women's right to vote was achieved, social reform would follow. However, a feminist backlash lasted until the eruption of the activism of the women's movement in the 1960s and 1970s.

The Depression Years

Hard times fell on the United States during the depression of the 1930s. Many lives were disrupted as men who worked in various types of heavy industry lost their jobs. Women who worked in the service sector saw little change in demand for their low-paying jobs, and were often found supporting their families through these lean depression years. Ironically, low-status jobs produced a positive economic position for working women and their families during the depression.

With the election of Franklin D. Roosevelt in the mid-1930s, the roles of women in America were elevated through the efforts of his wife Eleanor. She became a champion of women's and civil rights, and influenced the selection of the first woman ever to be appointed to a cabinet post. For the first time in history, women were allowed to work in United States post offices. Through the labor movement, gains in improved working conditions, minimum wages, and child labor laws came to fruition. Social Security was initiated, and the country was led out of the Great Depression only to be ushered into World War II.

World War II

The war brought thousands of women into the work force to replace the men who went off to war. Other women followed the men into the military and to war. They served their country as WAVES, WACS, SPARS, as nurses in the various services, and in support positions as Red Cross volunteers. Eventually, 400,000 women served their country in the various services as nurses, pilots, air traffic controllers, gunnery mates, instructors, meteorologists, messengers, intelligence officers, and in any other field where they were needed. However, they were subject to a strict code of conduct that prohibited a military woman from becoming inebriated, fraternizing with someone in the same service, and promiscuity (a relationship with someone outside the service). These limitations were repealed by the end of the war (Armas, 1994). Large numbers of women served on the front lines in the combat zones. Many gave their lives defending the nation, and some were captured and forced to spend years in concentration camps until they were liberated when the war ended. Despite their important role in the war, women were restricted from attaining rank higher than Colonel in the Army or Captain in the Navy (Armas, 1994).

At home, the ideal of American womanhood became Rosie the Riveter, who depicted women's important contributions working in defense factories (Banner, 1984). Litoff and Smith (1991) collected 30,000 letters that these women wrote to their husbands, brothers, and lovers who were serving overseas. These letters chronicled the transformation of the women who served in the factories on the home front. One woman wrote that she would never wash or iron again—laundries did that. Women had discovered a new sense of self and independence they had never experienced before.

When the war was over and the men returned, many women lost their jobs to make way for the returning war heroes. The majority of those women returned home to bear the children of the baby-boom generation, the largest this country has ever known. During this time it was typical for women seeking college educations to have the expectation of also receiving an "MRS degree." In other words, they chose to embrace marriage and raise a family rather than obtain a college degree. Frequently, coeds willingly dropped out of college to fulfill this expectation. Men, on the other hand, were expected to complete their education or to earn a living for the family. It was expected that husbands always perform their bread-winning role in the public sphere, while their wives were relegated to remaining at home to bear and rear the children (Banner, 1984).

During these years, the notion of suburbia was conceived. Suburban enclaves of tract homes on tree-lined streets were constructed and thousands of families bought the American dream house.

A new form of affluence emerged as families indulged their children with the things that they lacked in their own childhoods during the Great Depression. Dr. Benjamin Spock was embraced as the ultimate authority on how to raise children during the baby-boom generation era (Jones,

1981). Child-centered parents created the most privileged and indulged cohort in history. Contrary to the child-rearing experiences of their parents these children were both seen and heard.

The Baby-Boom Generation

Baby-boom children were the first to experience television and, for the most part, experienced more affluence than their parents. On the downside, since 76 million babies were born between 1946 and 1963, competition for a place in the world was tight (Jones, 1981).

These baby boomers were recognized by many contemporary researchers (Jones, 1981; Easterlin, 1980) as being unique, more liberal, and less conforming than those of the previous generation. As they reached adulthood, baby-boom women had more career and educational opportunities, later marriages, and more sexual freedoms than those who preceded them (Kessler-Harris, 1982). Some were among the first to experience the benefits of equal opportunity for women that resulted from the women's and civil rights movements. These women were socialized in an era of the sexual revolution with the advent of the birth control pill. Sexual activity was no longer delayed for fear of unwanted pregnancy. Many women openly participated in premarital sexual activity. Concurrent with all of these forces was the proliferation of illegal drug use, and the Vietnam protests. National self-doubt was rampant (Jones, 1981).

The Turbulent Sixties and Seventies

As the suffragettes influenced changes in women's rights, Betty Friedan (1963) is credited with instigating the unrest and, subsequently, the women's movement. She was instrumental in founding the National Organization for Women in the 1960s, and became famous for writing about the discontent in suburbia. Women, she wrote, were again relegated to a life of domesticity after experiencing freedom during the World War II era. She declared that societal expectations designated that the most appropriate roles for women were as mothers and homemakers. She, like Wollstonecraft, believed that women deserved the right to self-actualize and to achieve status outside the home, and that they were being prevented from doing so.

In 1981, however, Friedan reversed her views and stated that women were tired of the demands put upon them in the workplace. She claimed that women were once again turning to marriage and family to make their lives complete. She said that the feminist movement had swung too far to the left as a result of polarization by the abortion and gay rights issues.

The Eighties and Nineties

As a result of the activism in the 1960s and 1970s, women began to enter nontraditional occupations and education programs. However, women are still slow to achieve the same status as men in our society. Susan Faludi (1991) concurs that equality for women is still elusive. She reports that women represent 66% of all adults living in poverty. Women still earn only 70 cents of every dollar earned by men (Advertising Women of New York, 1993). This is seen as the worst gender pay gap in the Western world. Nontraditional professions still elude women. Eighty percent of working women are still relegated to traditional service jobs as nurses, secretaries, and salesclerks. In nontraditional positions as judges, lawyers, doctors, and corporate managers, women are still gravely under-represented.

Women's Bodies   Politicalization of the control over women's bodies still exists in the 1990s. There is great conflict and turbulence between pro-choice advocates and right-to-life groups over the abortion issue. This, in light of the fact that the issue was legislatively settled by the Supreme Court in the *Roe v. Wade* decision in 1973.

Strides are being made in awareness of violence against women. However, incidence rates of rape and other forms of brutality continue to climb. Many states still do not recognize marital rape, nor do they mandate arrest for battering during domestic violence incidents (Faludi, 1991).

Sexuality has taken an odd twist in the 1990s as a result of the AIDS crisis. The crisis, once thought to be limited to homosexual men, is now pervasive in the heterosexual society. HIV infection was the ninth leading cause of death for all persons in the United States in 1991. It was the third leading cause of death for men ages 25 to 44, and the sixth leading cause of death for women in this age group (Update, July 2, 1993). Until this preventable crisis is resolved, the spread of HIV and AIDS in women will continue to escalate. Programs that target intensive education about safe sex practices and that provide services such as clean needle exchanges for drug addicts must be explored and supported by both the government and society.

The Family   Marriage is still the preferred lifestyle for most Americans. According to Arthur Norton and Louisa Miller's 1993 report, 92.8% of all women ages 35 to 55 have ever been married. White women's marital experience is slightly higher (94%) than that of black women (84.6%), and Hispanic women (91.3%). In spite of the high rates of divorce, women in this same age cohort remarry at relatively high rates with 65.2% of all women choosing to remarry.

There is conflict among many married couples as the ranks of women in the work force swells to 57%. Many baby-boom women with lucrative careers are overloaded with the multiple roles of career, housekeeping, and parenting. Men, Faludi reports, still do not participate equally in household tasks and child-rearing (1991).

A growing trend is developing as former career women elect to leave their high-paying, nontraditional careers to return home to raise their families. A recent *Wall Street Journal* article, "Stay-At-Home Moms Are Fashionable Again" (Swasy, July 23, 1993), explains the phenomenon. Mothers who work outside the home are often made to feel guilty for putting their children in day care and for not volunteering in their children's school activities. At the same time, stay-at-home moms are voicing their resentment for having to bear the burden of becoming room-mothers and scout leaders for their own children while working moms do not contribute to their own children's activities.

Families with mothers at home demonstrate a marker of how well the family is doing. The position of stay-at-home mother is seen as a new status symbol, an indication that two incomes are not necessary to support the family. Some retired corporate executive women are so involved in volunteer activities and their children's lives that they report being just as busy as they were when they worked outside the home. Many have turned their homes into corporate-like models of efficiency and productivity. They claim that their children will benefit from a more hands-on type of parenting than from the previous day care arrangement (Swasy, July 23, 1993). It could be that these baby-boom mothers have become self-actualized in their earlier careers and are now content to achieve in motherhood. This may be construed as a new social norm for baby-boom women who have chosen later marriage and child-rearing.

Singlehood in the Nineties   Although one in four individuals in the United States lives alone, this is not a growing trend. Singlehood is accepted as an independent alternative to marriage. Putting off marriage until later in life may account for some of the single households. Elderly individuals who are financially independent and are living longer—many as widows and widowers—may help to explain the remainder of singles in this current but stable trend (U.S. Bureau of the Census, Current Population Reports, 1992).

Divorce   Divorce is pervasive in our society with one in four marriages ending in divorce in 1990. Between 1960 and 1980, the divorce rate doubled. One out of every two marriages ended in divorce. There was a small decrease in the late 1980s with no increases since that time (Norton & Miller, 1992). The baby boomers who put off marriage are now marrying and settling into family life and are producing a "baby boomlet" with an average of 2.1 children per family (U.S. Bureau of the Census, Current Population Reports, 1992).

In some instances divorce has brought about the feminization of poverty, with increasing numbers of women and their children living at poverty levels following divorce. The consequences of divorce have relegated women and children the poorest members of society, surpassing the elderly. This is due to a lack of commitment to child support and contemporary regard for the family structure. New legislation is, however, forcing delinquent fathers to pay child support or face imprisonment. The high teen pregnancy rate and subsequent single-parenting is also a contributing factor to this dilemma (Norton & Miller, 1992).

The Future

Many contrasts are evident in reviewing from an historic perspective. The 1990s are pivotal for the baby-boom generation, as they enjoy or first enter midlife. Neither the experiences they have had, nor their impact on the midlife transition, is well understood. Investigation and discussion of evolving behavioral norms and comparisons with the past are essential. It is hoped that this reflective exercise will aid in understanding midlife development in this significant cohort of the baby-boom generation. The ensuing chapters will describe lessons learned and further discussion of the complex issues surrounding women in midlife.

References

Advertising Women of New York. (1993). *Survey of men and women in advertising, publishing, and broadcasting*. New York: AWNY.

Armas, M.T. (1994). Women at war. *Naval History*. United States Naval Institute Publication, *8*(2), 10–14.

Banner, L.W. (1983). *American beauty*. Chicago: The University of Chicago Press.

Banner, L.W. (1984). *Women in modern America: A brief history*. New York: Harcourt Brace Jovanovich Publishers.

Easterlin, R.A. (1980). *Birth and fortune*. New York: Basic Books.

Faludi, S. (1991). *Backlash: The undeclared war against American women*. New York: Crown Publishers, Inc.

Friedan, B. (1963). *The feminine mystique*. New York: Dell Publishing Company.

Friedan, B. (1981). *The second stage*. New York: Summit Books.

Hochschild, A.R. (1983). *The managed heart: Commercialization of human feeling*. Berkeley: University of California Press.

Horowitz-Lefkowitz, H. (1984). *Alma mater*. Boston: Beacon Press.

Jones, L.Y. (1981). *Great expectations*. New York: Ballantine Books.

Kessler-Harris, A. (1982). *Out to work*. New York: Oxford University Press.

Litoff, J.B., & Smith, D.C. (1991). *Since you went away*. New York: Oxford Press.

McKinlay, J. & McKinlay, S. (1986). *Women and their health in Massachusetts*. Cambridge, MA: Cambridge Research Center.

National Center for Health Statistics. (1990). *Health, United States, 1989*. Hyattsville, MD: U.S. Public Health Service.

Norton, A.J. & Miller, L.F. (1992). *Marriage, divorce, and remarriage in the 1990s*. Washington, D.C.: U.S. Bureau of the Census. U.S. Government Printing Office, 1–21.

Rossi, A.S. (1973). *The feminist papers*. New York: Bantam Books.

Swasy, A. (1993, July 23). Stay-at-home moms are fashionable again in many communities. *The Wall Street Journal*. pp. 1, 4.

U.S. Bureau of the Census, Current Population Reports. (1992). *Marriage, divorce, and remarriage in the 1990s*. Washington, D.C.: U.S. Government Printing Office.

Update: Mortality attributes to HIV infection among persons aged 25–44 years; United States, 1990 and 1991. (July 2, 1993). *Morbidity and mortality weekly reports*. U.S. Department of Health and Human Services/Public Health Service. Atlanta: Centers for Disease Control and Prevention, 42(25), 481–486.

Chapter 2

Theoretical Discussion of Midlife Women

It has been reported that societal changes have rendered contemporary midlife women different from those who preceded them. However, numerous negative societal myths have been perpetuated because of a dearth of empirical studies on women in the midlife transition. To date, there is very little psychology, sociology, revisionist history, or coherent social science theory about women in this stage.

Conceptual Framework

The conceptual framework for this discussion is based on the psychosocial and developmental aspects of midlife identified in the existing literature on the midlife transition. Some of the major issues identified are as follows:

1. The potential of midlife women is only minimally recognized by society (Cahn, 1978; Gerber, Wolff, Klores, & Brown, 1989; Woods & Shaver, 1992).
2. Ageism and negative societal feelings can intensify fear of aging, health problems, and menopause (Doress & Siegal, 1994).
3. Women in midlife experience a generational pull in which children are making demands on one hand and aged parents are seeking assistance on the other (Light, 1988; Silverstone & Hyman, 1982).
4. The divorce rate for midlife marriages has increased dramatically with women between the ages of 35 and 49 leading the upward trend since 1985 (Norton & Miller, 1992). With the advent of multiple marriages, divorces, and remarriages there is an emergence of blended families, stepparenting, stepgrandparenting, and changing concepts of family configurations (Gerber et al., 1989).

5. There have been few noteworthy empirical studies of the midlife transition, especially as experienced by women. Among these is the ongoing Yale Midlife Study on Menopause (Sarrell, 1991), and the completed Massachusetts Women's Health Study (McKinlay & McKinlay, 1986) on the causes of menopausal stress. Since the baby-boom cohort of midlife women is currently entering the perimenopausal period, they have not been identified specifically in either of these studies.

6. As a group, those currently in the middle years are inherently different from those in previous generations who passed through this transition. This more articulate cohort demands and receives increased services and will probably work longer and be more involved in social action than others before them (Cohen & Gans, 1978; Gerber et al., 1989).

7. High anxiety levels and stress may not be present in midlife women as previously thought (Banner, 1993).

Many of these issues will be discussed later in this chapter and in other chapters of this book.

Developmental Theories

Erikson (1950) characterized midlife in terms of the conflict between generativity versus self-absorption. Generativity is described as raising one's family to adulthood and interacting with the older family members and grandchildren. According to Erikson, the individual in this stage is expected to extend the caring and concern aspects of generativity outside of the family for the welfare of the community at large. If Erikson's expectations for this life stage are not fulfilled, he believes that the individual will become self-absorbed and stagnant.

Stewart and Gold-Steinberg (1990) reached the conclusion that women's political consciousness in the middle years may be influenced by a preoccupation with generativity. A sense of satisfaction occurred when women in their study became politically active.

Batteson (1990) admonishes that even if an individual performs service and care it can be distorted if parenting becomes tyrannical, or if caring becomes dominating and bullying the powerless. It is imperative that these conflicts be successfully resolved in order to adapt successfully to the next life transition.

We must also question if the expectations put forth by Erikson should not be adjusted to accommodate the contemporary lifestyles of the baby-boom generation. Some of them are actually bearing children in their 40s and, in a few instances, other midlife women as old as 60. This was noted by Friedan (1981) when she chronicled a new type of raditionalism emerging in which there is a return to marriage and family values as women reach their late 30s and 40s. Aging parents, on the other hand, may still be engaged in the work force, and enjoy a long and relatively healthy life. For baby-boom midlife families, caring for older family members and grandparenting may be postponed. Erikson is mainly family focused, and does not take into account contemporary lifestyle choices. His developmental theory should be considered merely as one of the many frameworks available to examine the midlife transition.

Batteson (1990), daughter of well-known anthropologist Margaret Mead, offers us an interesting description and metaphor for the experiences of the pre-baby-boom generation of midlife women. She marvels at the forced creativity of herself and four friends, who are midlife and older, as they achieve despite their having to constantly adjust to changing environments. The oldest of the friends, Joan Erikson, is now in her 70s, and, ironically, is developmental theorist Erik Erikson's widow. Batteson describes the constant redefining of her life and the lives of her four friends. All are actively engaged in combining multiple roles that are always subject to interruption and improvisation. These women, along with most others in their generation, have been socialized to base their lives on the belief that when a woman is married she would take second place to her husband. As a result, the activities that women undertake in their lives are often undervalued by their families and society in deference to society's marital expectations. Sometimes, Batteson says, she has had difficulty taking her own worth seriously. She allowed her own work to be automatically interrupted when her husband called her for something. On the other hand, when she interrupted her husband he would finish his own task before responding to her request. Her response was always to defer to her husband. She goes on to recount moving her own career whenever her husband received a new assignment in a different location. There is an underlying resignation to what this has meant to her family and how they have benefited by her divided attention. She remains happily married.

Women have always been expected to shift from one activity to another, and to redefine and recreate their own priorities as a result of their social position. In terms of computer language, one could claim that women in our society are required to become parallel-batch processors because of their multiple roles and tasks. Men, on the other hand, have the option of completing one task before going on to another. One can only guess how much time will pass before this norm is reversed.

Increasingly, large numbers of midlife baby-boom women are reaching the top of the corporate ladder often requiring disruption of their families for *her* new assignment. As our society becomes increasingly diverse in every aspect we can only hope, like Batteson (1990), that the freedom to pursue more than one aspiration or role will be an emerging norm. In order to achieve this fantasy, the men in our society must be socialized to share in complementary and equal role participation. Faludi (1991), notwithstanding, does not give us much encouragement that marital and family expectations have changed significantly.

Gould (1978) suggested that midlife is a time of introspection in which the individual explores the prospect of his or her own mortality. He was influenced in part by Carl Jung (1961), recognizing the concept of inner uncertainty that prevails during the early stages of midlife. This is the time when childhood perceptions about what others think or do must be finally cast aside, and the focus becomes the self. In this self-discovery we become wiser and more philosophical. Moos (1977) adds that if an individual copes successfully with challenging life events, mechanisms for subsequent transitions are created. Gould's notion for developing a strong sense of inner self-directedness will buffer the pain associated with midlife issues such as divorce, chronic illness, forced retirement, job loss, ingratitude of those we love, and other tragedies. When we cannot resolve these conflicts, negativity and unhappiness will probably occur. This is a practical approach that is applicable to midlife development. However, it is essential that new developmental and theoretical approaches be formulated in order to understand and deal with our contemporary and dynamic environment.

Birren, Kinney, Shaie, and Woodruff (1981) reinforce the theories of Erikson, Gould, and Moos in their proposal that the manner in which individuals live their lives determines how long they will live as well as the quality of their lives. Accepting responsibility is a new dimension for midlife individuals as they must become well-versed in both the process of aging and their role in society. Managing stress and anxiety can help individuals to improve their life satisfaction and live longer lives.

Developmental psychology can enhance the prospects for increasing individual potential. It will evolve primarily from social and environmental sources rather than genetics. Through theoretical discussion, the issues that make the midlife transition the most pivotal of the life stages will be confronted.

Cohort Theory

Exploration of cohort theory is relevant so that the baby-boom and pre-baby-boom women may be compared to enhance our understanding of adult midlife development and transition. A cohort refers to an age group of people born during the same year or several year period (Jones, 1981).

Jennings and Nemi (1981) go on to describe a birth cohort as one that shares experience under somewhat similar circumstances. This creates a generational effect in which the individuals born during a similar time frame go through certain life adventures together. These life events take place at pivotal and impressionable times during early developmental phases before adulthood. It is logical to expect to find differences in attitude between the younger baby-boom cohorts, ages 35 to 48, and the older cohorts, ages 49 to 65, of midlife women. It is recognized that it is difficult to control an overlapping or "coat-tailing" effect as major life events simultaneously affect other cohort groups. Levels of maturity may also vary in individuals of the same age.

Similarly, it is challenging to understand the effect of change caused by aging in any study involving midlife women. One might theorize that the shared experiences of social change and upheaval that occurred during similar, pivotal times in the lives of the members of all of the cohort groups may be responsible for the overlapping of attitudes and feelings. It may become evident that shared experiences can affect attitudinal changes in life phases other than childhood and other pre-adulthood stages.

Previous Studies and Feminist Researchers

Previous studies on midlife were conducted mainly by men on dysfunctional women, based on Freudian theory (Freud, 1933). These studies reflected the perspectives of men who thought that any deviation from male behavior by women was pathological or neurotic (Bowles & Klein, 1983; Duffy, 1985). Freud portrayed women in midlife as pathological. He believed that women suffered from a castration complex that rendered them hysterical. This, he asserted, left middle-aged women craving sexual liaison with younger men. Feminist writers have refuted this theory as being narrow and not in the least representative of women in modern society.

Gilligan (1982) is credited with validating the psychological differences between men and women. In her research, conducted on adolescent boys and girls, she found that males viewed themselves in terms of autonomy and were threatened by intimacy. On the other hand, females tended to see the world in terms of connectedness and care. Women, she found, were often threatened by isolation and molded themselves to meet others' expectations and desires. The main premises derived from Gilligan's research are that women are less war-like than men, they do not play to win, and they become increasingly inhibited as they grow older. However, it is obvious that these findings cannot be generalized to all women. There is a continuum of behaviors that are attributable to each gender. Gilligan (1986) advocates additional studies of these differences as essential to under-standing the effects of social learning on psychological development in women. She contends that such eminent male researchers as Piaget, Kolberg, Levinson, Valliant, and Erikson left female subjects out of their developmental theoretical studies. They concluded that feminine behav-ior, according to their established behavioral norms, was deviant.

Banner (1993) concludes that the often touted midlife depression, cen-tral to Freudian theory, and the legendary empty nest syndrome that fol-lows child-rearing, are no longer relevant. As women have entered the work force they have become empowered and self-actualized. Other re-searchers have shown that women in their 40s and 50s demonstrate de-creased dependence, increased confidence, and decisiveness. It has also been shown that these women scored high on measures of coping, logical analysis, and tolerance for change. Menopause, the empty nest, and car-ing for aging parents did not cause discomfort or personality change for these midlife women. Change is attributed to long-term trends and matu-rity rather than life events (Helson & Wink, 1992). Rubin (1988) has also noted and confirmed these phenomena, as have other female midlife re-searchers (Jacobson, 1986; 1993).

However, myths about midlife depression and maladjustment con-tinue to be perpetuated. Recognition of the fact that women process dif-ferently than men is slow to emerge, as are changes in social norms. Pro-cessing in an alternative mode does not signify depression or deviance (Faludi, 1991).

Furthermore, Gerber, Wolff, Klores, and Brown (1989) reported that there were virtually no scholarly books or studies written by gerontolo-gists that covered midlife through old age until the early 1980s. As a con-sequence, we have no body of proven, repetitive patterns of midlife de-velopment to explain how individuals make the transition through the various stages in midlife. It appears that the popular press and others are still not convinced of the scientific findings that have come forward.

Feminist Theory

Feminist theory may yield still another mechanism to theorize about midlife development in women. It relates to women from an holistic per-spective within a societal context. However, some are critical of the fact that feminists have not addressed the changing demographics that relate to the needs of an emerging older population of women (Pohl & Boyd, 1993). Feminists, they claim, are concerned simply with women in the workplace, as well as those experiencing motherhood, reproductive rights, and relationships with men. Certainly, these objections have some validity. It should be recognized that even in light of these criticisms the feminist movement has made some major contributions to women's lives. The feminist contribution in enhancing women's self-worth in society should not be trivialized or discounted.

Three types of feminists are now described. Liberal feminists were instrumental in heightening awareness about the inequalities experienced by women in the workplace and other societal institutions. They have undertaken the task of correcting these injustices in terms of a growing trend toward equal wages for equal work, and the emergence of women into male-dominated professions. The struggle continues, but there is slow progress in meeting these goals.

Radical feminists have raised our consciousness about the oppression of women throughout society. They have a very narrow perspective, viewing all women as a homogeneous group (Pohl & Boyd, 1993). This restrictive focus, with its emphasis on reproductive rights, eliminates the individuality of all other women. It is obvious that for women who choose not to bear children, menopausal women, and older women, reproductive issues may be of peripheral interest. It is the radical feminists, according to Friedan (1981), who may have undermined the liberal cause toward equality. They have been champions of abortion and gay rights, and negative attitudes toward males whom they view as the oppressors. Their efforts splintered the feminist movement as many middle-of-the-road women retreated from the feminist movement.

Ehrenreich (1983), a social feminist, speaks of social constructs in society in which the expectations are for men to be the breadwinners while women follow the patterns of early marriage and child-rearing. Chodorow (1978) suggests that men can also nurture and participate in child-rearing. In their description of societal structure, it is clear that the orientation is basically concerned with the division of labor between women and men primarily in the childbearing phase of the life cycle. The consequences for older women as they encroach on the sequential stages in life are not fully explored. It will be important to incorporate and understand inequities in dealing with women in all stages of the life cycle. We hope this will facilitate political awareness that will culminate in beneficial public policies for women, regardless of age.

Characteristics of Baby-Boom Women (Ages 35 to 48)

The baby-boom generation, born after January 1, 1946, has been referred to in various ways. Harold Hodgkinson, Director of the Center of Demographic Policy, made reference to an embarrassingly long victory celebration following World War II (Personal Communication, November 5, 1992).

Jones (1981) likened this cohort to a pig moving through a python. Job market competition and vying for limited spaces inspired this generation to promote themselves. They became increasingly entrepreneurial, seeking their place in society. Independence and the self-help movement were the themes of this birth cohort as they searched for happiness. As a result, this generation was also labeled the "me generation." They wanted the best of everything and were used to instant gratification (Jones, 1981).

The Vietnam generation is still another term attributed to this cohort that numbers 76.4 million men and women born between 1946 and 1964 (Statistical Abstract of the U.S., 1985). According to the research findings in *Enduring Legacies* (1987), this designation incorporates the events that occurred during the years between 1963 with the assassination of President John F. Kennedy, and 1972 with the second inauguration of President Richard M. Nixon. During these years the civil rights movement occurred, as did the Vietnam War, anti-war protests, the women's movement, the establishment of the Peace Corps, the sexual revolution, the explosion of drug and rock music cultures, and the assassinations of Robert Kennedy and Martin Luther King, Jr. (*Enduring Legacies*, 1987). In this study, the newest cohort of 954 midlife individuals reported that they were:

1. Moderate to conservative on economic issues;
2. Idealistic and proponents of social justice, somewhat anti-establishment;
3. Social and political activists;
4. Increasing participants in the corporate world, as they head in the direction of conservatism;
5. Shifting values with regard to self-fulfillment and acceptance of diversity, especially in regard to sexuality;
6. Increasing numbers of women participating in the workplace, married and with young children and working both inside and outside the home, often referred to as the double day;
7. Users of computers and other high-tech equipment both at home and the office.

A sense of hope for the future and a determination to make it happen was expressed by the participants (*Enduring Legacies*, 1987). The respondents appeared to be more spiritual than organized in their religious beliefs and honest leadership was an important value. Other feelings defined were concern over the AIDS epidemic, a decline in moral values, and the alienation pervasive in society. Some in the study believed that midlife transition was a move away from their former hedonistic attitudes toward an increased social awareness.

Jones (1981) chronicled the baby-boom generation before it became middle-aged. His is a view of a troubled, hedonistic me generation. He portrayed a sick society with rising suicide rates, drug and alcohol abuse, and the emerging self-help movement in which everyone is obsessively searching for individual happiness. This aggregate is seen as having lost confidence in itself and the country as a whole. The baby boomers were off to an auspicious beginning, having been offered the best of everything as their parents became increasingly affluent. What went wrong, according to Jones, is linked to the enormous size of the baby-boom cohort. This has led baby boomers to a stressful and competitive life involving long working hours and uncertainty about the future. They found that they could not equal the living standards of their parents once they were on their own. However, baby boomers have solved the problem through such alternate schemes as dual-career families, and postponement of marriage and child-rearing until these aspirations could be reached.

A breakdown in the family system, along with rising divorce rates among their own midlife parents, added to their disillusionment. The recurring question regarding a lack of leadership or direction for the country, following the assassinations of the 1960s, has also contributed to the unhappiness expressed by this generation.

It should be taken into account that all midlife women are not the same. Pre-midlife baby boomers, still in their early 30s, differ from early and later midlife baby boomers (ages 35 to 48), and each of these groups exhibit differences when compared with pre-baby-boom women (ages 49 to 65). Based on Faludi (1991), the characteristics of each of the cohorts are somewhat distinct, although some may overlap as a result of societal norms and pressures.

Characteristics of the Youngest Cohort of Midlife Baby-Boom Women (Ages 35 to 40)

1. They have not experienced as many of the limitations with regard to sexuality, education, career, and marital choices as their older counterparts.
2. They have rarely expressed militancy in their beliefs about feminism.
3. They still cherish family values, but have put off marriage and child-rearing more than any other cohort.
4. Educational and career opportunities have opened up for them, except in the case of those who have been affected by the recession and have lost their jobs.
5. Many claim that they will never be as affluent as their parents. However, they stand to inherit the affluence accumulated by their families.

6. Instant gratification and lack of patience are making some of them unhappy.
7. They are computer literate.
8. They are dealing with the AIDS crisis.

Characteristics of the Oldest Cohort of Midlife Baby-Boom Women (Ages 41 to 48)

1. They were in the vanguard of the feminist movement. Some of them participated in the Vietnam protests and the civil rights movement.
2. They were active participants in the sexual revolution and were the first generation to have access to the birth control pill.
3. They espouse family values, but have put off marriage and child-rearing and have smaller families than those before them.
4. They have a higher divorce rate than their older counterparts, but are remarrying and raising blended and reconstituted families.
5. Many have been somewhat active in nontraditional careers. It has been shown that women are not choosing nontraditional careers despite educational opportunities open to them.
6. Their household income is equal to that of their older counterparts, but only because they live in two-income households for the most part.
7. They were raised with Dr. Spock's values in child-centered households and have been called the self-centered me generation, demanding and getting what they want instantaneously.
8. They were raised in front of the television set.

(Faludi, 1991; Jones, 1981; and Naisbitt, 1982).

They are consumers of the first order, and even go so far as to present their own birthing plans when they bear children. They demand the best of everything. Huge amounts of monetary resources, probably due in part to their advocacy, are finally being allocated to the study of women's health. They have changed every institution that they have touched because of the need to expand to accommodate them.

The future has been and will continue to be shaped by this large cohort. As this group shifts into retirement age, it is predicted that all government systems will become strained if no solutions are found to assure the integrity of the social security system. Many baby boomers fear that they will never receive any benefits from the social security system. In reality, however, this group will demand and receive increased services, and will probably work longer to receive these benefits than any cohort before them.

On the positive side, having had so many educational advantages will ultimately contribute to a healthier old age. The baby boomers are expected to practice healthier lifestyles as they age because of their preoccupation with self-fulfillment and happiness. It is important to realize that they are consumers of the first order, and the recipients of the most advanced medical and technological advances.

Jones (1981) ends on an upbeat note as he discusses what he feels are some positive effects of being a member of this overwhelming generation. He foresees an increased tolerance for a broad range of nontraditional lifestyles, increasing tolerance for minorities, and reform of our institutions resulting from daring to question authority. Finally, he projects the enhancement of women's rights. In spite of a somewhat tarnished image, the baby boomers will succeed and find their place in the world. Since a baby boomer was elected President of the United States in 1992, Jones could be considered a visionary.

Cohen and Gans (1978) add that baby boomers will pursue lifelong learning activities that are both stimulating and meaningful. Many will have changing and varied careers. Multiple marriages will be the norm because of the high divorce rate. Due to the lengthening of the life span, it is expected that there will be an increase in multigenerational families. This may necessitate additional family responsibilities, placing even greater stressors on the midlife baby-boom generation.

Greenhouse (1993) conducted a survey on her 1968 graduating class from Harvard University on the occasion of their twenty-fifth reunion. This class was among the first wave of baby boomers to graduate from college. They were portrayed as opinionated, brash, and anti-establishment. It appeared that everything that the generation preceding them believed in was contrary to their beliefs. They wanted to implement change in society. Surprisingly, after 25 years, it appears that this cohort has been transformed into active and successful members of the establishment. However, there remains a hint of rebellion, as reflected in some of their liberal political views. For example, most claimed they voted for the democratic ticket in 1992, with 91% of the women in the survey voting for Clinton versus 69% of the men. True to their former liberal convictions, abortion rights and handgun control were overwhelmingly favored by all members of the class.

In an attempt to avoid any generalizations about the pre-baby-boom cohort of older midlife women, I have divided them into two groups. This should allow you to understand the discriminate differences between the two arbitrarily divided cohorts.

Characteristics of Older Pre-Baby-Boom Women (Ages 59 to 65)

No discussion of the baby-boom generation of midlife women would be complete without some explanation of those who preceded them in this phase of the life cycle. Lowenthal, Thurner, and Chiraboga (1975) were among the earliest theorists to report on the lack of a framework for studying the midlife transition. They attempted to study the effects of this stage by investigating lifestyle configuration, complexity of self-image, models of adaptation, and continuity between values and goals. This was the first systematic approach to assess the extent of adaptive processes in adults. Structural dimensions of marriage were also studied. Among other things, their studies revealed that the demands of motherhood limited participation in activities outside the home for this cohort. This led them to realize the vast differences between the activities of women and men.

With the passage of time, roles changed as the children became older and more self-sufficient. Women at this juncture became more involved in community activities. The middle-age lifestyle appeared to focus on occupational roles as women in this group prepared for the post-parental stage. Marital dissatisfaction, in this study, was found to be most prevalent in midlife marriages compared to all other cohorts.

Rubin (1979) substantiates this finding. Lowenthal et al. (1975) found that, in general, middle-aged women had very negative self-images. Furthermore, they displayed greater unhappiness and absentmindedness than women in other stages of life. It was also found that neither the empty nest nor menopause seemed to be causing stress in these midlife women. Rather, these researchers claimed that the main cause of stress in these women arose from unhappiness with their spouses. There appeared to be a general absence of new life events as changing roles emerged. In general, it was established that midlife women were in a more critical state than men in this age group. The women in this study felt that they had been kept from their goals. In working to meet their husbands needs and societal expectations, they perceived a lack of options in the outside world. Lowenthal et al. concluded that a lifelong learning perspective needed to be integrated into midlife women's lives. This would serve to diminish the large proportion of frustrated and self-deprecating adult women. It was thought that this would help midlife women prepare for the later stages of life. It is important to mention that Lowenthal, a male researcher, sampled only a small number of midlife women. His findings should be critically assessed.

No doubt, these were the women so aptly described as languishing in suburbia as their husbands went off to attend to the important tasks in society (Friedan, 1963). They remained at home taking care of the children and the household chores. During this era, it was widely believed that careers and higher education would lead to the masculinization of women and would have detrimental effects on both the home and children. So, women remained at home to produce and raise the baby-boom generation. This continued until Friedan's book sold over a million copies. Unrest was created in suburbia and the women's movement was born. The new desires and goals for women were self-actualization, a demand for equality, and educational opportunities so long denied.

Other researchers characterized the cohort of women born in the 1920s and 1930s as having served in traditional roles, known war, experienced increased government control, raised children and grandchildren, lived in suburbia, and observed the heavy workloads that their husbands carried to sustain their large families. This cohort has seen inflation, increased technology, and many in this cluster have returned to college to prepare for empty nest productivity (Burnside, Ebersole, & Monea, 1979).

In an oral history account, Harvey (1993) interviewed a group of midlife women who are now in their late 50s and 60s. They recalled that the only real choice for women in their cohort when they came of age during the 1950s was marriage and family. The underlying fact was that women were continuing to enter the work force following World War II. They increased the ranks of working women by the mid-1950s from 16 to 22 million. However, women's work outside the home was viewed as trivial, simply providing a supplement to the family income. The extra funds allowed luxuries such as family vacations, college tuition, and other nonnecessities. Frequently, these women encountered hostility on the job and, if they returned to school, in educational institutions.

Older midlife women faced many other paradoxes in their lives. Halas and Matteson (1978) wrote that women were dominated by men who made all the decisions and rules. Women served in subordinate roles which were shunned by men. Women were expected to facilitate men's lives and were responsible for raising the family and homemaking. When women in this era worked outside the home, they were often criticized for neglecting their families, rather than admired for helping with the family finances. Assertiveness was a problem for these women. They had to learn how not to say yes when they meant no. This was a problem because it was considered unfeminine to express anger or refuse others' demands. They were socialized to believe that they were responsible for pleasing and giving to others. Husbands were not usually supportive of their wives' self-actualization yearnings. Faludi (1991) contends that a successful woman, to this day, is usually seen as a negative influence by the male segment of society.

A somewhat unfavorable representation of middle-aged women was described in Self's research (1969), encompassing 2,000 middle-aged women from suburban Detroit. Three similar characteristic commonalities of his subjects were pervasive lack of confidence, depression stemming from perceived loss of youth, and an identity crisis. The identity crisis is the manifestation of long years of sacrifice experienced while caring for children and supporting their husbands' occupational advancements. These women were left with a loss of direction and feelings of loneliness and isolation. Some expressed guilt because they did not encounter happiness after attaining the American dream in suburbia with all of its advantages. When a woman did venture outside the home, she might fear that her husband's ego would be damaged if she accomplished too much and became aggressive and unfeminine.

On the other hand, Self reported that when a woman became successful in this era, there was a sense that the rest of the family would benefit from her growing self-esteem and happiness. Women in this stage were given a choice to become neurotic and self-destructive or, paradoxically, to grow in their environment through the self-actualization process. His explanation is tantamount to the typical confusion and double messages repeatedly given to midlife women.

In 1978, Levinson presented a conceptual framework to study the middle years that he felt had been sorely neglected until this point. He suggested study from three constructs:

1. the individual's sociocultural world;
2. conscious and unconscious self; and
3. participation in the world.

Many of the earlier midlife theorists related their findings to males, except in the instance of Levinson's 1978 study, when the above framework was applied to a small sample of women. This study finally produced the notion of credibility for studying midlife women and opened the door to additional, more conclusive studies.

Rubin (1979) is credited with one of the most comprehensive investigation of what she termed *women of a certain age*. She questioned 160 women from diverse backgrounds who were ages 35 to 54. According to her study, few of the women had experienced the empty nest syndrome. Most actually breathed a sigh of relief when their children left home. They reported loving their children but, nevertheless, ready for life without them. Rubin explains that fathers, not mothers, experience the most distress when the children leave home. Fathers suddenly realized that the children have matured and that things would never be the same again. It is as if suddenly, before they had a chance to participate in their upbringing, the children were grown. Conversely, women who participated in the traditional role of homemaker had the luxury of experiencing each and every landmark event in their children's lives. During the 1970s and 1980s men were expected to be the achievers, while women were raised to be pretty, kind, and loving wives and mothers.

Volunteer work was an acceptable pursuit for women in traditional roles, while working for pay outside the home was not. It is suggested that as volunteers, women did not offer any threat to their male counterparts. Men, Rubin reported (1979), were threatened by powerful women who could support themselves. When women did work outside the home, however, they were still expected to perform household chores. Men usually did not participate in mundane tasks around the house. It is interesting to note that as some midlife women were gearing up in meaningful work outside the home, some of their husbands were looking forward to early retirement, while others were lowering their own career expectations. Rubin explains that women in this midlife cohort lived the first half of their lives vicariously through their families, and were now on the verge of a new identity.

Characteristics of Younger Pre-Baby-Boom Women (Ages 49 to 58)

These women were born during the mid-1930s and the 1940s and are distinguished as having had increased options compared to those born earlier. They were described in terms of living in the nuclear age, exploring the moon, receiving increased educational opportunities, and achieving affluence and abundance. These women have emerged to be less traditional than those in the previous cohort. The youngest women in this cohort, born before the baby boom in 1946, are identified as the television generation. They were visually oriented and among the first to have watched war on their living room television sets (Burnside et al., 1979).

It is astonishing to think of the strides that midlife women have made since these early reports. Today, this creativity and vigor experienced by many midlife women is often recognized with awe and admiration. Vitality is now an option for most midlife women as they enjoy newfound freedoms. Batteson (1990) reminds us that it can only occur if, in composing our lives, we continuously reimagine the future and reinterpret the past to give meaning to the present. We must remember best those events that prefigured what followed, forgetting those events that proved to have no meaning (Batteson, 1990, p. 30).

Contemporary Research Efforts

In a landmark longitudinal study, the husband and wife team of McKinlay and McKinlay (1986) interviewed 2,500 midlife women ages 45 to 55 over a five-year period to analyze changes in family status, health, and work.

They found, as did other contemporary researchers, that depression is not necessarily a result of the menopause or widowhood during the middle years. Empty nesters were actually out working, or otherwise happily involved in activities outside the home.

Mitchell and Helson (1990) conducted a study of 700 female college alumnae ages 26 to 80 years. In addition to the 700, a longitudinal study of 118 women who were 43 in 1981 and 52 in 1989 was also included. The major finding in this study was that women in their early 50s rated their quality of life as high. Both samples of midlife women at this time in their lives experienced better health, higher income, and reported increasing concern for their elderly parents. They perceived that they were in the prime of life, secure, confident, and involved in numerous interesting activities.

On the horizon of research on the development of relevant midlife theory is the news of a launching of a center for Women's Health Research supporting the study of women's biopsychosocial health across the life span. Initially, the center will focus on midlife and older women, and will be funded in part by the National Center for Nursing Research. The center is housed at the University of Washington, where a group of nurse researchers have combined their collective talents in the scholarship and training of other researchers. In describing the center, Woods and Shaver (1992) note that since the 1970s, nurses have been in the forefront of advancing scholarship and research on women's health. They cite The First International Congress on Women's Health in Halifax, Nova Scotia, as a watershed event providing a forum for scholarship on women's health. I was given the opportunity to present an earlier research study on midlife women with military spouses at this event (Jacobson, 1986). Since then, the proceedings from the conference and other research about women's health, both nationally and internationally, have been published in the journal *Health Care For Women International*. Phyllis Stern has edited and inspired the journal since it was started in the late 1980s.

Banner (1992) has given an historical feminist perspective on aging women that will stimulate further investigation. The gigantic baby-boom cohort of aging women will greatly influence this stage in the life cycle as it continues to seek truths and answers about its own mortality and place in the life cycle.

The next chapter will build on some of the issues presented in this theoretical discussion, while also discussing health and psychological issues in midlife women. In Chapter 4, I will present an in-depth account of a study that was conducted in 1989 to compare midlife baby-boom women to their older counterparts in midlife. Many of the issues discussed here will be replicated in the discussion of my research on the midlife transition in women.

References

Banner, L.W. (1992). *In full flower*. New York: Vintage Books.

Batteson, M.C. (1990). *Composing a life*. New York: The Atlantic Monthly Press.

Birren, J.E., Kinney, D.K., Shaie, K.W., & Woodruff, D.S. (1981). *Developmental psychology*. Boston: Houghton Mifflin.

Bowles, G. & Klein, R.D. (1983). *Theories of Women's Studies*. London: Routledge & Kegan Paul.

Burnside, I.M., Ebersole, P., & Monea, H.E. (1979). *Psychosocial caring throughout the lifespan*. New York: McGraw-Hill.

Cahn, A.F. (1978). Highlights on eighteen papers on problems of midlife women. In *Women in Midlife*. Select Committee on Aging. Washington, D.C.: U.S. Government Printing Office (COMM. Pub. No. 95–170).

Chodorow, N. (1978). *The reproduction of mothering*. Berkeley: University of California Press.

Cohen, B.J., & Gans, B.M. (1978). *The other generation gap*. Chicago: Follett.

Doress, P.B., & Siegal, D.L. (1994). *Ourselves, growing older*. New York: Simon & Schuster.

Duffy, M.E. (1985). A critique of research: A feminine perspective. *Health Care for Women International, 4*, 341–352.

Ehrenreich, B. (1983). *The hearts of men*. Garden City, NY: Anchor Books.

Enduring legacies: Expressions from the hearts and minds of the Vietnam generation. (1987). Washington, D.C.: Center for New Leadership.

Erikson, E.H. (1959). *Childhood and society*. New York: W.W. Norton.

Faludi, S. (1991). *Backlash*. New York: Crown Publishers, Inc.

Friedan, B. (1963). *The feminine mystique*. New York: W.W. Norton & Company, Inc.

Friedan, B. (1981). *The second stage*. New York: Dell Publishing Co., Inc.

Freud, S. (1933). *Femininity: New introductory lectures on psychonalysis*. New York: W.W. Norton.

Gerber, J., Wolff, J., Klores, W., & Brown, G. (1989). *Lifetrends: The future of baby boomers and other aging Americans*. New York: Macmillan.

Gilligan, C. (1982). *In a different voice*. Cambridge, MA: Harvard University Press.

Gilligan, C. (1986, Winter). Reply by Carol Gilligan to critics. *Signs, 6*, 325–333.

Gould, R.L. (1978). *Transformations*. New York: Simon & Schuster.

Greenhouse, L. (1993, June 10). They're back for their 25th reunion. *The Boston Globe*, p. 63.

Halas, C., & Matteson, R. (1978). *I've done so well—why do I feel so bad?* New York: Macmillan Publishing Co., Inc.

Harvey, B. (1993). *The fifties: A woman's oral history*. New York: Harper Collins.

Helson, R., & Wink, P. (1992). Personality change in women from the early 40s to the early 50s. *Psychology and Aging, 7*(1), 46–55.

Jacobson, J.M. (1986). A comparison of anxiety levels in midlife women (aged 35–65) who are military spouses and a group of non-military affiliated women. *Health Care for Women International, 7*, 241–253.

Jacobson, J.M. (1993). Midlife baby boom Women compared with their older counterparts in midlife. *Health Care for Women International, 14,* 427–436.

Jennings, M.K., & Nemi, R.G. (1981). *Generations and politics.* Princeton, NJ: Princeton University Press.

Jones, L.Y. (1981). *Great expectations.* New York: Ballantine Books.

Jung, C.G. (1961). *Memories, dreams, reflections.* New York: Random House.

Levinson, D.J. (1978). *The seasons of a man's life.* New York: Alfred Knopf, Inc.

Light, P.C. (1988). *Baby boomers.* New York: W.W. Norton.

Lowenthal, M.F., Thurner, M., & Chiraboga, D. (1975). *Four stages of life.* San Francisco: Jossey-Bass Publishers.

McKinlay, J., & McKinlay, S. (1986). *Women and their health in Massachusetts.* Cambridge, MA: Cambridge Research Center.

Mitchell, V., & Helson, R. (1990). Women's prime of life: Is it the 50s? *Psychology of Women Quarterly, 14*(4), 451–470.

Moos, R.H. (1977). *Human adaptation.* Lexington, MA: D.C. Heath and Company.

Naisbitt, J. (1982). *Megatrends.* New York: Warner Books.

Norton, A.J., & Miller, L.F. (1992). *Marriage, divorce, and remarriage in the 1990s.* Washington, D.C.: U.S. Bureau of the Census. U.S. Government Printing Office, 1–21.

Pohl, J.M., & Boyd, C.J. (1993). Ageism within feminism. *Image: Journal of Nursing Scholarship, 25*(3), 199–201.

Rubin, L. (1979). *Women of a certain age.* New York: Harper & Row.

Sarrell, P.M. (1991). Women, work, and menopause. In M. Frankenhaeuser, U. Lundberg, & M. Chesney (Eds.), *Women, Work, and Health: Stress and Opportunities.*

Self, G. (1969). *Search for fulfillment: Women on the move.* A paper presented at the Governor's Commission on the Status of Women. Las Vegas, Nevada.

Silverstone, B., & Hyman, H.K. (1982). *You and your aging parent.* New York: Pantheon Books.

Statistical Abstract of the United States. (1985). Washington, D.C.: U.S. Department of Commerce, Bureau of the Census.

Stewart, A.J., & Gold-Steinberg, S. (1990). Midlife women's political consciousness. *Psychology of Women Quarterly, 14*(4), 543–566.

Woods, N.F., & Shaver, J.F. (1992). The evolutionary spiral of a specialized center for research on women's health. *Image: Journal of Nursing Scholarship, 24*(3), 223–228.

Chapter 3

Significant Concerns for Midlife Women

Health and Psychological Concerns

The numerous factors that affect women in midlife are discussed in this chapter. It is my goal in writing this book to emphasize that menopause is not the overriding issue in every discussion of the midlife transition in women. In most instances, we are led to believe that the menopause is the major cause of physiological and psychological distress for midlife women. The panacea of using medical solutions, with very little consideration of possible long-term effects or other alternatives, is often considered to be the sole remedy. I believe that the most pressing issue for midlife women is to become informed of the health and psychological issues that will confront them in this stage of life. Erikson (1950) says that we must come to terms with the issues in each life transition in order to continue on successfully to the next stage. Numerous significant issues are presented in this chapter. Others, more contemporary issues, will be explored in Chapter 5.

The literature regarding medical treatment and options for a variety of normal and abnormal conditions affecting midlife women will be discussed. I do not wish to devalue the enormous contribution that the medical profession has made to the general well-being of society. It is essential, however, to recognize that there is an overwhelming lack of medical and scientific knowledge concerning women's health issues. It is imperative that women, especially those in midlife, become consumers in control of their own medical care. Too many women submit to the opinion of a single physician without question. They are often forced to make decisions with too little information about their condition and the wide range of options available. It is essential for women to be aware of the principles of self-care as they educate themselves about health problems and all available choices. In the case of impending surgery of any kind, an unbiased second opinion should always be sought. It is important to take the time to compare alternatives in order to make informed decisions. In life-threatening situations when immediate action may save a life, this is not possible.

Cancer

Cancer is one of the leading causes of death in midlife women, second only to heart disease (Boring, Squires, & Tong, 1992). In a startling research study Davis, Dinse, and Hoel (February 9, 1994) report that white men and women in the baby-boom generation are 80% and 50%, respectively, more likely to develop some form of cancer than their ancestors born during the later decades of the nineteenth century. While death from cardiovascular disease has declined over the past four decades, the risk for developing cancer has risen. White baby-boom men had two times the cancer rate for all cancers of men born between 1888 and 1897. Baby-boom women had a 50% increased rate for all cancers. In addition, the baby-boom women exhibited a 30% higher rate for cancer, due to smoking, when compared to women born between 1888 and 1897. Breast cancer rates for baby-boom women increased at twice the rate of the comparison group. The number of individuals with newly diagnosed cancer incidence during a 15-year period was obtained from the Surveillance, Epidemiology and End Results Program (SEER) database, in cooperation with the United States Census Bureau. These data were collected through the SEER program from various geographic areas in the United States, representing a cross section of roughly 10% of the population. Boring et al. (1992) report that breast cancer accounts for 16% of all cancer deaths, while ovarian and uterine cancers account for 5% and 4% respectively (Davis et al., February 9, 1994).

It was also reported that the data for minority groups, in the older cohorts, were found to be unreliable. The only positive findings are that treatment modalities and early detection have prevented the high mortality rates that were previously noted. It was concluded that the increase in cancer rates is not necessarily linked to aging, diagnostic patterns, or smoking behaviors. This is true except in the case of lung cancer, which is directly attributed to smoking, and accounts for 22% of all cancer deaths (Boring et al., 1992).

The findings are comparable to those from a Swedish study by Adami, Bergstrom, and Sparen (1993). Because all of the cancers, except lung disease, were not attributed to specific etiologies, the researchers were led to determine that carcinogenic environmental sources may be linked to these grave findings. They report that exposure to unspecified carcinogens in the environment may be a contributing factor to the higher rates. These findings may have far-reaching implications in the quest for the causes of many cancers, including breast cancer. Further studies of pathogens in the environment like insecticides, fertilizers, and other substances in our food and water must be seriously undertaken. Through this intense effort, possible carcinogens will be identified. This knowledge will allow us to prevent further instances of cancer.

Breast Cancer

One in eight women in the United States will develop breast cancer over the course of a lifetime. In 1940, the risk was 1 in 20. In 1960, it was 1 in 14, and as late as 1987, it was 1 in 10 (National Cancer Institute, September, 1992). In 1994, estimated cases of breast cancer among American women rose to 182,000, the highest incidence of any type of cancer in women (American Cancer Society, 1994). Mortality from breast cancer is shocking: one woman dies of breast cancer every 12 minutes. In 1994 alone 46,000 women will die of this dreaded disease. Women are dying of breast cancer at the same rate today as they were in 1930. This is second only to lung cancer which resulted in the deaths of 59,000 women in 1994 (American Cancer Society, 1994). To treat women with breast cancer, the medical and scientific community has developed magnificent treatment regimens. These measures are not only costly in terms of dollars, but the mental anguish is priceless. In any event, a nonbinding assurance of only five additional years of longevity is all that can be offered to most victims. Some lucky individuals survive past five years, given the breast lesion was discovered at an early stage and there is no lymph node involvement or metastases to the other parts of the body such as the lungs and bones. To anyone who has lost a relative or dear friend in the prime of life to this devastating disease, there is little or no consolation. Until recently, with concerted efforts like the Women's Health Initiative (Cotton, 1992), scant resources have been allocated to identification of causative agents either through epidemiological or bench research. It appears at this point in time that researchers have provided us with numerous expensive treatments and diagnostic modalities that give us very little hope for prevention or a long-lasting cure.

It is also surprising that so little attention has been focused on the investigation of the factors that tend to protect Asian women from developing breast cancer in their country of origin. An epidemiological investigation of the factors that tend to keep Asian women from developing breast cancer in their own countries should be undertaken. When these women emigrate to the United States and adopt the American Lifestyle, they manifest rates of breast cancer similar to those of American women (Osteen, Connolly, Costanza, Harris, Henderson, & McKenney, 1990).

Willett and Hunter (1993) agree that breast cancer rates vary around the world, and that daughters of immigrants appear to adopt the rates similar to those of their adopted country.

Recently, at The Center for Cancer Risk Analysis at the Massachusetts General Hospital Cancer Center in Boston, the current status of the Breast Cancer Susceptibility Project was described. The researchers identified a breast cancer gene, BRCA1, that is responsible for 5% of all breast cancers. It was reported that there are presently five research groups throughout the country attempting to clone the gene. The University of Utah recently announced that their team had accomplished the task. Numerous other genes have also been identified that are linked to colon. ovarian, and thyroid cancers. In addition, the discovery of the presence of susceptibility or trigger genes that must be present to allow the development of a cancerous tumor was illustrated (Friend, March 29, 1994). It is only through the support of this type of scientific exploration that we will be able to conquer this devastating plague.

Dietary Risk Factors for Breast Cancer   Willett and Hunter (1993), in their longitudinal lifestyle study of over 100,000 nurses, have been conducting epidemiologic studies on the role of dietary practices in developing breast cancer. They suggest that limiting intake of fat to 20% of the total diet may protect against breast cancer. Thus far, the relationship between fat intake and breast cancer has proven inconclusive, but the eight-year study is ongoing. Nevertheless, researchers suggest that decreasing dietary fat intake is beneficial not only for cancer prevention, but also for protection against cardiovascular disease. It appears that we all should be reading food labels and limiting fat intake. Furthermore, high-fat diets are also implicated in the development of high blood cholesterol levels and subsequent heart disease. As early as 1985, in a case-control study, Lubin, Ruder, Wax, and Modan (1985) looked at 1,065 Israeli women with breast cancer. As a result of this study, it was established that being overweight was positively related to the risk of breast cancer in older, postmenopausal, women. It is important to note here that breast cancer incidence is higher in women over age 50 (American Cancer Society, 1994) than in younger women, and that dietary fat may be incidental to development of breast cancer. These women, however, were also noted to be consumers of high-fat diets. In 1986, Wynder, Rose, and Cohen cited epidemiologic evidence strongly suggesting that dietary fat, with the possible exception of olive oil, plays an important role in the pathogenesis of breast cancer. In a more recent study, Mills, Beeson, Phillips, and Fraser (1989) describe the influence of diet on breast cancer risk among Seventh Day Adventists. This religious group was chosen for study because they are typically vegetarian and consume an average of

8.6% of their daily calories from animal fat. This is in contrast to 24.3% reported for the general population. On average, fat comprises 36% of Seventh Day Adventist individuals' total calorie intake, while most other Americans consume 42.6% of total calorie intake as fat (Mills et al., 1989). The connection between fat intake and breast cancer is a consistent finding despite erroneous press reports that the issue has been settled to the contrary (Rennie, January/February, 1993).

Vitamins   Willett and Hunter (1993) studied the effects that the daily intake of vitamins A, E, C, and selenium had in relation to their protective effect against developing breast cancer. But again, these studies are inconclusive. It is somewhat puzzling that in my survey research of dietary risk factors for breast cancer, the majority of the women diagnosed with breast cancer did not take daily doses of vitamins (Jacobson, 1994). Longitudinal studies on the effects of daily vitamin intake are ongoing and should be supported to determine if a preventative link to breast cancer exists. Many physicians advise women that if they eat a well-balanced diet, vitamins are not necessary. However, most women in this fast-food world do not have a well-balanced diet.

Alcohol   A strong link to breast cancer has been associated with alcohol consumption. Although the literature relating breast cancer risk and alcohol consumption remains somewhat contradictory, recent cohort studies seem to confirm that a strong link to alcohol intake is in some way related to breast cancer development (Graham, 1987).

Schatzkin, Jones, Hoover, Taylor, Brinton, Zeigler, Harvey, Carter, Licitra, Dufour, and Larson (1987) investigated the link between alcohol consumption and breast cancer risk in 7,188 women. These women were participants in the first National Health and Nutrition Examination Survey (NHANES I). This epidemiologic study followed a cohort of women over the course of ten years. During this time, 121 were diagnosed with breast cancer. It was found that consumption of any amount of alcohol was associated with an overall increased risk of breast cancer of up to 50%. The greatest risk (40–50%) occurred in those women who consumed more than five grams a day, or the equivalent of three drinks a week. The association between drinking and breast cancer was stronger among younger, leaner, and pre-menopausal women according to the NHANES I study.

Willett, Stampfer, Colditz, Rosner, Hennekens, and Speizer (1987) report from data in the Nurses' Health Study. In this stage of their cohort study of 89,538 women, it was found that breast cancer is approximately 59% more likely to develop in women who consume alcohol. The opposite is true for women who drink little, less than five grams a day, or who drink no alcohol. Similar findings were recorded by Schatzkin et al. (1987) who also demonstrated that the risk was dose related. In their study, those who drank more than five grams of alcohol a day demonstrated an increased risk (30–60%) for developing breast cancer over those who drank little or no alcohol.

As is the case with other reported risk factors for breast cancer, additional epidemiologic studies are needed in order to clarify the relationship between alcohol consumption and breast cancer. A study conducted by Webster, Wingo, Layde, Lee, Rubin, and Ory (1993) discounts the above studies that link alcohol consumption and breast cancer. They examined Centers for Disease Control data from the Cancer and Steroid Hormone Study, a case-control study of 1,226 women with confirmed breast cancer, and found no relationship between alcohol consumption and breast cancer. Obviously, there is still inconclusive evidence and further study is essential.

Family History   Women with a family history of breast cancer are at increased risk of developing breast cancer. There is such a strong correlation that Carter, Jones, Schatzkin, and Brinton (1989) identified family history as the major risk factor for developing breast cancer. Ottman, King, Pike, and Henderson (1983) have confirmed this risk factor using a set of probability tables. Most sources agree that a history of breast cancer in a first-degree relative, mother or sister, places a woman at a statistically significant risk for the disease (Brinton, Hoover, & Fraumeni, 1983). Roseman, Straus, and Shorey (1990) point out that this is especially relevant for women under 60 years of age. Sattin, Rubin, and Webster (1985) revealed that women with a first-degree relative with breast cancer had a 2.3-fold higher risk for developing breast cancer. Those with a second-degree relative, aunt or grandmother, with breast cancer had a 1.5-fold greater risk. A woman's risk was 6.5 times greater if both her mother and sister had breast cancer. Cases of breast cancer attributable to family history was lowest for women ages 20–39 and highest for those ages 45–54.

Lipnick, Speizer, Bain, Willett, Rosner, Stampfer, Belanger, and Hennekens (1984) in a case-control study of 844 breast cancer cases discovered a 90% increased risk in pre-menopausal women if their mothers had a history of breast cancer, and a 200% greater risk if they had a sister with the disease. Roseman et al. (1990), in their case-control study of 9,000 women, demonstrated that family history is a breast cancer risk determinant only for women under the age of 60. After 60, the odds of a woman with a positive family history developing breast cancer are no greater than in a woman with no family history. It should be noted that the vast majority of women diagnosed with breast cancer have no family history of the disease. In a related study by Rohan and McMichael (1988), women with a family history of breast cancer had substantially increased risk for breast cancer if they used exogenous estrogen therapy.

The Tamoxifen Debate   No discussion of family history and its relationship would be complete without mention of the Tamoxifen studies started in 1992. This enormous Breast Cancer Prevention Trial is heralded by the National Cancer Institute (NCI) as a primary prevention measure to prevent breast cancer in women at high risk because of family history. The 68 million dollar study encompasses 270 centers in the United States and Canada. The study personnel will recruit 16,000 women with the appropriate risk factors over a two-year period. The study will continue for five years. Half of the women are being treated with daily dosages of 20 milligrams of Tamoxifen while the other half, the control group, will receive a placebo. Similar studies are also under way in Great Britain, Italy, and Australia. The NCI has supported the trials because it believes that the incidence of breast cancer will be reduced by one-third. An added benefit of reducing cardiovascular disease by 30% and reducing fracture due to osteoporosis is also cited (Fugh-Berman & Epstein, 1992; Bush & Helzlouer, 1993).

However, there are serious concerns regarding the study expressed by the authors noted above and numerous women's advocacy groups. Tamoxifen is a synthetic nonsteroidal agent that has been widely used as an adjuvant treatment for breast cancer. The drug has been found to limit recurrence of the disease mainly in women who are over fifty years of age. The drug limits the production of estrogen in the body and has been said to reduce osteoporosis and cardiovascular disease in women who have had breast disease (Bush & Helzlouer, 1993). The rationale for the trials was based on findings mentioned above when data from women with breast disease showed the incidence of one-third fewer tumors in the unaffected breast when Tamoxifen was prescribed. Fugh-Berman and Epstein (1992) and Bush and Helzlouer (1993) question how this rationale can be projected to healthy women. The anticipated subjects will be women who do not have breast cancer, or are not post-menopausal, as some participants in the trials did have breast cancer or were post-menopausal. They go on to report other data that offers weak support for the protective qualities of Tamoxifen on bone mass and cardiovascular disease. Constructive criticism by these researchers is directed toward the National Cancer Institute regarding this primary prevention trial that has raised many serious questions.

The Tamoxifen study criteria includes all women over 60 and women ages 35 to 59 who demonstrate risk factors equivalent to a 60-year-old woman. The risk factor criteria are age, number of first-degree relatives with breast cancer, age at menarche, and age at first live birth. All women who have had lobular carcinoma of the breast with surgical removal are also invited to participate in the study. The study will exclude all women who are pregnant or intend to become pregnant, use oral contraceptives, and use hormone replacement therapy. Women who report past use of Tamoxifen, a history of ductal carcinoma of the breast, or a history of invasive breast cancer are also excluded (Bush & Helzlouer, 1993). The risk factors attributed to Tamoxifen are identified as endometrial cancer, thromboembolic disease, retinopathy, and liver cancer. Other potentially serious side effects are hot flashes, depression, vaginal discharge and dryness, and irregular menses with little protection against unwanted pregnancies in pre-menopausal women. These dangerous side effects may be acceptable for women who have been diagnosed with life-threatening breast cancer, but healthy women should consider whether participating in the Tamoxifen study is worth the possible risk to their overall health.

Bush and Helzlouer (1993) warn that the harmful effects of the drug are undervalued in the net-benefit equations. Women who participate in the study may actually be harmed and more than likely will receive no benefits. As a result, the use of Tamoxifen as a primary prevention strategy is flawed because of the toxicity of the drug and its unknown, potential side effects. Arguments such as cardiovascular protection, because the drug has been found to reduce low-density lipoprotein cholesterol lipids, are questioned because the drug's effect on the major lipid protector in women is not clearly defined. The risk for endometrial cancer in women with intact uteri is well documented. However, the participants are simply advised to have routine annual checkups, rather than annual endometrial biopsies. This is accounted for by the dubious assumption that endometrial cancer is relatively easy to treat. However, the authors report that recent findings have shown that women treated with Tamoxifen are at risk for high-grade endometrial cancers that are not associated with positive prognosis. Not providing for regular monitoring with endometrial biopsy is also seen as a major flaw in the study by these authors.

Bush and Helzlouer (1993) also admonish that the risk for serious embolism may be increased fivefold in women being treated with Tamoxifen. Lastly, the authors are concerned about the risk for liver cancer. Studies from Great Britain have shown numerous cases of liver disease among Tamoxifen users. In addition, because of the possibility of ocular involvement in women being treated with Tamoxifen, regular systematic eye examinations should be provided for the subjects. These researchers are voicing grave concern as to whether the Breast Cancer Prevention Trial should continue in its present form. They contest that limiting the trials to women over 60, when most women are at risk for breast cancer, might lend credibility to the study. The major argument against the trials is that treating large numbers of healthy women with a toxic substance, under the umbrella of primary prevention, should not continue.

Gynecological and Reproductive History   Korenman (1980) proposes an explanation for the relationship between hormones and breast cancer that focuses on the length of a woman's exposure to hormones and the critical times of life during which a woman is exposed to carcinogens. The estrogen window hypothesis provides one explanation for the increased risk of breast cancer associated with recognized hormone-related events in a woman's life.

Estrogen Window Hypothesis

1. Human breast cancer is induced by environmental carcinogens to a susceptible mammary gland.
2. Unopposed estrogen stimulation is the most favorable state for tumor induction.
3. There is a long latent period between tumor induction and clinical expression.
4. The duration of exposure to estrogens determines risk.
5. Susceptibility to tumor induction declines with the establishment of normal luteal phase progesterone secretion (p. 700).

According to the hypothesis, becoming pregnant offers some protection against breast cancer because of changes in the mammary gland during the second half of pregnancy. The later the first pregnancy, the longer the duration of the open window, and the greater the risk.

Data from the Nurses' Health Study (Lipnick, Speizer, Bain, Willett, Rosner, Stampfer, Belanger, & Hennekens, 1984) support the estrogen window hypothesis. Women in the study who reported giving birth for the first time after age 35 had a 40% increased risk of developing breast cancer. No consistent association was found between age at menarche and breast cancer. There appeared to be some protective effect in women who had a history of multiple normal pregnancies. Brinton, Hoover, and Fraumeni (1983) note that nulliparity, generally associated with increased risk, was not predictive of breast cancer risk in their study conducted during the Breast Cancer Detection Demonstration Project sponsored by the National Cancer Institute. It was concluded that pregnancy does not reduce breast cancer risk. As in other studies, a woman's risk of breast cancer increased, however, if she gave birth for the first time after age 30. These findings were replicated by Carter, Jones, Schatzkin, and Brinton (1989). However, Carter et al. (1989) did find a higher incidence of breast cancer in women who did not become pregnant. Age at menarche of 15 and older was found by Brinton et al. (1983) to confer a 34% lower risk for breast cancer than for women whose menstrual periods began before age 12. Carter et al. (1989) did not concur on this finding which precipitates the need for additional correlation studies.

Oral Contraceptives   Epidemiologic evidence suggests there is some evidence of an association between a woman's hormonal status and her risk of breast cancer. The role of oral contraceptives, a combination of estrogen and progestogen, and breast cancer risk was investigated by Vessey, Doll, Jones, McPherson, and Yeates (1979). In this study of 707 women an association between oral contraceptive use and breast cancer in women ages 46 to 50 was noted. Because the findings were not consistent in other age groups, they were believed to have been related to chance.

In a Swedish study conducted by Olsson, Ranstam, Baldetorp, Ewers, Ferno, Killander, and Sigurdsson (1991), a significant relationship between early oral contraceptive use and the risk of pre-menopausal breast cancer was observed. Early teenage history of contraceptive use yielded a high risk factor for breast cancer. In general, early oral contraceptive users were found to have larger tumors and a poorer survival rate than women who did not have an early history of oral contraceptive use. These findings may be attributable to the higher dosages that were used in earlier oral contraceptives.

In contrast, earlier studies by Miller, Rosenberg, Kaufman, Schottenfeld, Stolley, and Shapiro (1986) demonstrated no apparent increase in breast cancer risk with long-term oral contraceptive use up to age 45. It is interesting to note that the long-term latent effect may yet be unknown. In 1988, Schlesselman, Stadel, Murray, and Lai also found no support for a long-term latent effect of oral contraceptive use on breast cancer risk through age 54. In another study involving a meta-analysis of oral contraceptive use and breast cancer, no significant association was determined (Romieir, Oberlin, & Colditz, 1990).

Benign Breast Disease   In relation to a woman's history of benign breast disease, Rohan and McMichael (1988) found no positive association between estrogen use and increased breast cancer risk. However, Brinton et al. (1983) observed a high risk of breast cancer among women who had both ovaries removed and used estrogens in the presence of a benign breast disease. Similar findings were obtained by Ross, Paganini-Hill, Gerkins, Mack, Arthur, and Henderson (1980) when they associated risk of breast cancer development with high total milligram accumulated dose of conjugated estrogen among women with a prior history of surgically diagnosed benign breast disease. The women in these earlier studies did not have the benefit of progesterone to protect against endometrial cancer (Sobel, 1994).

Early Detection   Screening mammography contributes to early detection and longer survival rates in women over 55 (Anderson, Aspergren, Janzon, Landberg, Lindholm, Linnell, Ljungberg, Ranstam, & Sigfusson, 1988). Liff, Sung, Chow, Greenberg, and Flanders (1991) conducted a study to determine if the increased mammographic screening accounted for the rising incidence of breast cancer. However, because more breast cancer was being detected because of increased access to this diagnostic procedure, it was established that increased screening only partially accounts for the rising incidence of breast cancer in the United States.

The current recommendations of the American Cancer Society (ACS) in *Cancer Facts and Figures*, 1994 call for universally applied population screening to detect breast cancer and reduce mortality. Women are advised to perform monthly breast self-examination and to have an annual breast examination by a health care professional. In the study by Rohan and McMichael (1988), the incidence of breast cancer was found to be higher among women who failed to practice breast self-examination. Women ages 40–49 are advised to have a biennial mammogram, and those ages 50 and older to have an annual mammogram. Mammography is not recommended for women under age 40 unless they have family risk or other factors warranting early mammography. The reason cited for this is that breast tissue is more dense prior to age 40, rendering unreliable mammographic results. The ACS stresses the importance of both mammograms and breast self-examinations because mammography still fails to find 10% of breast tumors. Innovative strategies like Magnetic Resonance Imaging, Ultrasound, and Positron Emission Tomography scanning for axially nodes (PET), are being implemented to assist in the earliest possible detection (Hulka, 1994). This discussion becomes a moot point when we examine the lack of access to these advanced technologies for poor and uninsured women who are also at extremely high risk for breast cancer (Kirkman-Liff & Kronenfeld, 1992).

Cardiovascular Disease

Heart disease is also a major cause of concern for both baby-boom women and their older counterparts in midlife. The American Heart Association (1993) states that when all heart and blood vessel diseases are combined, they claim the lives of around 485,000 women each year. This is not only a disease of the elderly, as more than 161,000 individuals under age 65 die of heart disease every year. One in nine women ages 45 to 64 has some form of cardiovascular disease. Stroke, rheumatic heart disease, and hypertension are included in the classification of cardiovascular disease. According to the American Heart Association (1993), 6,000 women will die of heart attacks each year, and more than 25% of them will be under age 45. Black women are 1.4 times more likely than white women to suffer deadly heart attacks.

Risk factors for cardiovascular disease that cannot be changed are aging, being male, and family history. Those that can be changed are lifestyle choices such as smoking, which yields 2–4 times the risk of disease. Oral contraceptives combined with smoking present an even greater risk of heart attack. The risk becomes 22 times more for women who smoke and use oral contraceptives simultaneously. It appears that women in the menopausal years are at greater risk for heart disease than younger women (American Heart Association, 1993). However, Sobel (June, 1994) reports that many of the studies regarding cardiovascular disease have been predicated on males and projected onto women, rendering them inaccurate.

Recent studies have explored the high mortality rates reported for women with coronary heart disease (Ayanian & Epstein, 1991). It was found that female heart attack victims are receiving unequal treatment in comparison to male heart attack victims. Physicians often withhold surgical treatment, diagnostic procedures, and other interventions when dealing with female patients. One probable explanation is that accepted medical interventions for cardiovascular conditions have been based on interventions used when males present heart attack symptoms. More often than not, these interventions have proved inadequate, or are ineffective when applied to women.

In a retrospective analysis of coronary artery bypass and angioplasty, Ayanian and Epstein (1991) estimated 28% more bypass surgeries, and 15% more angioplasty procedures were performed on men than on women. They state that there are systemic and anatomical differences, such as smaller diameter vessels in women, that may mitigate the effectiveness when the procedures are applied to female patients. It is interesting to note that these procedures have led to the decline in death rates from cardiovascular disease for men. Evidence of these differences in treatment is important, and the benefits should be carefully considered when applying treatments to female patients. Frequently, advanced procedures have been offered to women in an advanced stage of disease and they have produced little more than poor prognoses and high mortality rates.

In describing the subjects in the study above, it was found that there were nearly 50,000 hospital discharges, of which 45.9% were females older than the men in the sample. The women were predominantly non-white, insured, and had primary diagnoses of unstable angina, and secondary diagnoses of congestive heart failure and diabetes mellitus. These female patients were less likely than the males to have myocardial infarct or chronic ischemic heart disease (Ayanian & Epstein, 1991).

In the ensuing discussion, Ayanian and Epstein (1991) suggest that advanced procedures may be overused in male patients and underused in female patients. It is suggested that these advanced procedures may be offered primarily to men because they suffer higher incidence of heart disease than women. Apparently, when women present with distinct and advanced symptoms of heart attack (myocardial infarct), their fatality rates are higher than in male victims. It has also been noted that when coronary bypass is performed on women it is less effective and more often fatal than it is for males. Perhaps this is another consideration in the explanation of the discrepancies between males and females.

Angioplasty also yielded poorer results and relief from symptoms for women than men in the study. The anatomical structure of a vessel is normally narrower in women than in males and may further explain the rationale for withholding the procedure. Ayanian and Epstein (1991) also suggest that preference for surgery may be lower in women who often choose medical treatment and adjusting activities instead. However, the authors concede that access to the above procedures may be unequal, and not offered as an option for many female cardiovascular disease victims.

McElmurry and Parker (1993), in their review of women's health, concur with the above findings. They note that, although there is increased attention given to women and heart disease, the knowledge base remains male dominated. This may result in a bias in the diagnosis and treatment of women with symptoms. The authors project that in the future a greater understanding of women's unique diagnostic and treatment requirements, with regard to coronary diseases, will be better understood. They conclude that primary preventive strategies such as diet, smoking cessation, and exercise will be major factors in improving the growing incidences of heart disease in women as they age.

Menopause

It is obvious from the previous and ensuing discussions that there are numerous issues of a more immediate nature than menopause that affect women in the middle years. Nevertheless, the menopause is an important issue that must be discussed, and information should be made readily available to all women. It has, in some instances, been overemphasized by societal expectations and mythical thinking.

Various definitions have been used to describe the normal physiological process of menopause. One of such definitions is described by Sloane (1985) as the final phase of a woman's reproductive ability. It refers to the cessation of menstrual periods and is considered complete after one year of amenorrhea. The physiological changes may be either gradual or abrupt. Climacteric is the period when the declining ovarian function eventually terminates in complete menopause. The onset is believed to be influenced by age at menarche, race, heredity, climate, nutrition, general health, and socioeconomic status (Jenson & Bobak, 1985; Sloane, 1985). Ten percent of women experience the menopause around age 40, but for most women 50 is the average age. Another 5% of women may wait until age 60 before the menopause occurs.

Physiology of Menopause

Menopause is characterized by changes in the production of various hormones. Ovarian activity decreases during the menopause, and a decline in the production of ovarian hormones occurs. The decreased hormone production causes increased secretion of leutinizing hormone (LH) and follicle stimulating hormone (FSH) from the pituitary gland. Within a year of menstrual cessation, the FSH level increases up to 13 times, the LH level up to three times the normal levels expected during the reproductive years. Declines are also noted in the levels of ovarian estrogen and progesterone (Sloane, 1985).

Hormonal changes during menopause bring about a variety of signs and physical changes. Some women experience uneventful menstrual cessation, while others may experience severe reactions that are occasionally disabling. These may include vasomotor flushes, hot flashes, thinning of the vaginal lining, nervousness, poor memory, depression, insomnia, dizziness, bloating, nausea, and loss of bone mass.

Physical Changes During the Menopause

1. Normal aging attributes, such as a few more wrinkles.
2. Dry skin.
3. Thinning of the bones in sedentary women (due to medical condition or lifestyle choice) who do not take supplementary calcium, or in women who have a family history of osteoporosis.
4. Thinning of the vaginal tissue (atropic urogenital changes).
5. Period of peripheral nervous system instability causing hot flashes in some women, maybe as high as 75% of menopausal women. Although only 25% report symptoms to physicians, only half of these have symptoms severe enough to be medicated.
6. Some women report fatigue and occasional sleep loss because of hot flashes. Lack of sleep may be attributed to causes other than the menopause.

Psychological Changes During the Menopause

Depression in midlife women, when it is reported, has been attributed to several causes, some mythical. Some are listed below.

Menopause Myths (Based on Banner, 1993; Doress & Siegal, 1994; and others listed below)

1. All women in midlife become depressed and neurotic.
2. The change of life is an illness.
3. If a family member suffered from depression, you will inevitably experience depression.
4. Loss of worth to society.
5. You will become sexually ugly and unappealing.
6. Your bones will become brittle and will dissolve.
7. Memory loss.
8. Insomnia (everyone may suffer from loss of sleep at one time or another, but it is not necessarily attributable to the menopause).

Plausible Occurrences During the Menopause

1. Divorce.
2. Biological illness begins (osteoporosis, cancer, diabetes, etc.).
3. Death of a spouse, parents, or a child.
4. Caring for aging, sick parents.
5. Effects of aging: wrinkles, weight gain, etc.
6. Alcoholism in self or a family member.
7. Adolescent children's problems.
8. Balancing work and family roles.
9. Misinformation or no information about the menopause.
10. Fear.
11. Unsympathetic family.
12. Negative societal expectations and portrayal.
13. Empty nest syndrome (mythical for most, but plausible for some women who have not been able to refocus and redirect their lives).

New Social Norms for an Emerging Majority of Midlife Women

1. Post-menopausal zest.
2. Independence.
3. Well-groomed, beautiful midlife women.
4. Newfound self-confidence.
5. Menopausal women engaged in careers.

6. Upbeat and youthful midlife women enjoying their children and grandchildren.
7. The perception that menopause is an insignificant issue for many women who deny severe symptoms and consider the menopause a natural transition.

(Based on findings of the following: Campbell & Whitehead, 1977; Nachtigall, Nachtigall, Nachtigall, & Beckman, 1979; Sloane, 1985; Doress & Siegal, 1994; Batteson, 1990; McElmurry & Parker, 1993.)

In summary, menopause is not an estrogen-deficiency disease. Rather, it is technically a hypoestrogenic state (Sobel, 1994). We have tended to overuse medical approaches. Few women are informed of the fact that the adrenal glands gradually take over some of the production of non-ovarian estrogens and that there are alternatives to medical interventions. Many of the uncomfortable side effects may be alleviated if a peri-meno-pausal woman participates in activities such as weight-bearing exercise at least three times a week. Other healthy lifestyle practices and diet are also instrumental in allaying menopause symptoms. Vitamin supplements, such as vitamins B and C, are also recommended. Severity of symptoms has been related to the inhibiting of the production of non-ovarian estro-gen. It appears that reducing the intake of alcohol, caffeine, and sugar may actually result in a decrease of hot flashes, nervousness, and other symp-toms attributed to the menopause (Doress & Siegal, 1994; Boston Women's Health Collective, 1992).

Hormone Replacement Therapy

Rosenberg (1993) claims that physicians have medicalized the menopause by offering hormone replacement therapy (HRT) to millions of American women, sometimes for life. Widespread use began in the 1970s when large dosages of estrogens were prescribed unknowingly to thousands of women who subsequently developed endometrial cancer. The use of es-trogen replacement therapy (ERT) became unpopular until lower dosages were prepared that included progestin, to preclude the uterine cancer in women with intact uteri. Currently, unopposed estrogens are prescribed for women who have had hysterectomies. Rosenberg claims that some phy-sicians are still prescribing unopposed estrogens, whether or not a woman has an intact uterus. Despite the fact that periodic endometrial biopsy is recommended in women with intact uteri who use unopposed estrogen therapy, many women are not informed about this precaution. The author suggests that adding progestin may not protect against cardiovascular disease and may, in fact, be associated with the development of breast cancer. The data on the cardiovascular benefits of estrogen plus progesterone are inconclusive. According to Sobel (1994), earlier studies combining estrogen and progesterone revealed that opposing effects lowered the cardiovascular benefits of estrogen when progesterone was added. Newer forms of progesterone may prove beneficial in offering cardiovascular benefits. Several foreign studies, and the ongoing Women's Health Initiative (Cotton, 1992), may prove promising and eventually substantiate the benefits of progesterone (Sobel, 1994). In the meantime, alternative therapies are available that address both cardiovascular and skeletal health. The critique of HRT is heroically presented by Rosenberg (1993) because of the frequent and accepted practice of prescribing HRT by the medical profession. Few authors have been uninhibited enough to suggest that HRT needs to be reevaluated. Rosenberg (1993) ponders why so little attention has been focused on promoting other strategies. Too often, the benefits of higher bone density, decreased menopausal symptoms, and protection against heart disease when unopposed estrogens are prescribed are heard loud and clear.

The argument that has been put forth for so long regarding the beneficial effects of HRT in protecting bone mass may be somewhat mitigated as well (Felson, Zhang, Hannan, Kiel, Wilson, & Anderson, 1993). It was reported that it takes at least seven years for the effects of estrogen on bone mass to be detected. What has been found is that women 75 and older who have been treated with HRT benefit only slightly more than older women who have not been treated with estrogen (Felson et al., 1993).

Rosenberg (1993) claims that there are numerous unanswered questions about HRT. We do not have clear guidelines on how long estrogens must be taken, whether the effects diminish after discontinuing, what doses are effective, and who can benefit. The claim regarding cardiovascular protection is also questioned. Healthy women who do not have cardiovascular disease are included in the studies on the benefits of HRT. Rosenberg questions the fact that studies separating healthy subjects from those with existing heart disease have not been conducted. Since Rosenberg's work is mainly an issues paper that includes a compilation of current research, her position cannot be scientifically supported. However, the questions she raises are poignant. Longitudinal studies must continue to be conducted on women using alternative methods before we can support or discount the use of HRT.

Rosenberg also states that the long-term effects of HRT must be monitored closely so that we can have conclusive answers to what is the most beneficial intervention for menopausal women. Women who are contemplating HRT must be well educated on both the benefits and risks of this menopause treatment. Alternative methods should also be presented and considered.

Most studies have demonstrated that unopposed estrogens reverse the thinning of the urogenital area. Observational reports and laboratory findings have substantiated protection against osteoporosis and cardio-vascular disease. The risk factors, however, remain ominous.

Unanswered Questions

- How long must estrogens be taken for the benefits to take effect?
- How soon after the HRT is discontinued do the effects dissipate?
- What are the proper dosages?
- Who should take HRT? Not all women can. They are contra-indicated in some types of vascular conditions such as migraine headaches. HRT may also increase the risk of thromboembolic disease. They should not be used by women who have had breast cancer or any other type of cancer (Rosenberg, 1993).

Considerations

- Unopposed estrogens can cause uterine cancer long after the use of HRT is terminated.
- Women with intact uteri who use estrogens for long periods of time should be monitored through endometrial biopsy. This procedure is sometimes quite painful and can be expensive. Few women involved in HRT submit to this procedure and many are not encouraged to do so (Rosenberg, 1993).
- Some studies indicate that long-term use causes breast cancer. Steinberg, Thacker, Smith, Stroup, Zack, Flanders, and Berkle-man (1991) investigated the relationship between the duration of estrogen use and its effect on breast cancer risk by combining data from several studies in a meta-analysis. Breast cancer risk increased after at least 5 years of estrogen use. After 15 years, there was a 30% increase in the risk of breast cancer (relative risk factor 1.3 with a 95% confidence interval of 1.2–1.6).
- Some forms of estrogen, such as estradiol, may be more harm-ful than others in causing breast cancer (Bergkvist, Adami, Persson, Hoover, & Schairer, 1989).
- Estrogen with progestin can have side effects such as menstrual breakthrough bleeding, bloating, and depression.
- Little is known about the long-term effects.
- Although there is emerging data that may support the benefi-cial effects of HRT, there is conflicting evidence on cardiovas-cular effects (Sobel, 1994).
- Progestin added to estrogen may increase lipids and thereby increase risk of cardiovascular disease.
- There are emerging studies on the effects of estrogen on fibrino-gen, blood pressure, and glucose tolerance.

- The benefit–risk ratio varies with age. Breast cancer is a more important cause of illness and death for younger women. In older women, studies of protection against cardiovascular disease are inconclusive because some women who take estrogens are healthy and do not have risk factors for heart disease. Basing cardiovascular claims on this statistical inference may prove unreliable in claiming protection when no risk was present.
- There is a tendency for wealthy, well-educated women to use HRT that may result in overestimating the risk of breast cancer. On the other hand, women at high risk for breast cancer may avoid estrogen. Risk may be underestimated.
- Studies of HRT that include progestin are not conclusive for risk of cardiovascular disease and breast cancer.

(Based on Rosenberg, 1993 and studies mentioned previously in this chapter)

Rosenberg (1993) reports there are three trials now in progress regarding HRT. The Estrogen/Progestin Intervention Trial, in which a random grouping of peri-menopausal women are given estrogen alone, estrogen with progestin, or a placebo. The subjects will be followed for three years. During the period, surveillance of high density lipoprotein blood levels, glucose tolerance, fibrinogen, and blood pressure readings will be ongoing. Another study is in a Secondary Prevention Trial conducted on women who have survived heart attacks in order to determine whether or not estrogen will offer protection against repeated myocardial infarction. The third trial is the Women's Health Initiative, under the umbrella of the National Institutes of Health. In this project, women are chosen at random to receive either HRT or placebo for a nine-year period. In addition to blood studies, repeated myocardial infarcts, fractures, and cancers will be closely monitored. Unfortunately, we will not know the results of any of these studies for many years.

Previously, HRT was prescribed for short periods of time to allay menopausal symptoms. More recently, it has been prescribed for indefinite periods of time. In a survey of Los Angeles gynecologists, it was reported that almost all prescribed HRT for menopausal women. Both estrogen and progestin were prescribed, whether their patients had intact uteri or not (Rosenberg, 1993).

Colditz, Stampfer, Willett, Hennekens, Rosner, and Speizer (1990), Steinberg et al. (1991), and Rohan and McMichael (1988) demonstrated that the longer the duration of hormone replacement therapy, the higher the increase in risk of breast cancer. These studies are substantiated in a study of 23,244 Swedish women over the age of 35. An increase of 10% in relative risk for breast cancer was revealed in women who were taking estrogen. The risk increased to 70% when the hormone was taken for over 9 years (Bergkvist, Adami, Persson, Hoover, & Schairer, 1989). Further, the use of estradiol, a potent estrogen, was found to double a woman's risk after 6 years of use. Weaker estriol preparations were not associated with an increased breast cancer risk. In this study, the addition of progesterone to estrogen replacement therapy (ERT) appeared to offer no protection against the development of the disease.

The Boston Women's Health Collective (1992) warns that there may be a 30–50% higher risk for developing breast cancer in women using HRT. Women must be informed and advised of the risks of long-term use of hormone replacement therapies, and nonmedical approaches must be investigated. There are no easy answers. There may be long-term effects after seven to ten years of estrogen intake, however, we really do not know enough about the cardiovascular effect. The benefit to the cardiovascular system may be valid if a woman is without a uterus and has a family risk factor for osteoporosis. Densitometry, however, has not been effective in screening for hip and vertebral factors. Again, there are large gaps in knowledge of estrogen and progestin therapies (Rosenberg, 1993).

One can only guess whether or not physicians are unnecessarily prescribing estrogen and progestin therapies. Why not use antihypertensive drugs, and other drugs specific for heart disease, to allay cardiovascular symptoms in patients who are at risk? Has the medical profession been cavalier or naive in prescribing HRT? Doctors collectively tell us that the risk of developing osteoporosis outweighs the risk of preventing breast or uterine cancer even though most women do not require estrogen to overcome menopause symptoms. Studies like the one conducted by Zhang, Feldblum, and Fortney (1992) should be considered. These researchers observed 352 peri-menopausal women who used personal activity computers to measure their physical activity. They found that moderate physical activity, the burning of 100 calories a day in physical activity, increased spinal bone mineral density significantly.

Sheehy (1991), noted for her characterization of midlife issues in the popular press, has also portrayed the menopause mainly from a medicalized perspective. She relates the benefits of the use of estrogen replacement therapy as a balm that leads to increased sexual libido and freedom from the perils of aging in midlife women. She implies that women who do not take HRT are no longer sexual and sensuous, and are not protected from heart disease and osteoporosis. Putting women at high risk for uterine cancer is simply discarded by Sheehy because "there is a high cure rate for uterine cancer that is caught early" (p. 203). Sheehy concludes that the HRT debate will continue to rage as the baby boomers make their way into the menopause years. She appears, however, to stress a somewhat unbalanced point of view. While she offers alternatives, she gives the impression that HRT is the preferred option. Had she been a little more evenhanded, this would have been a more credible resource for midlife women. The overall message is that women should be aware of all of their options and then consult with their physicians or nurse practitioners to examine the benefits and risks of HRT.

Aburdene and Naisbitt (1992) present a more evenly balanced case. They state that Premarin (estrogen) is the second most prescribed drug with sales over $569 million in 1991 (p. 154). They examine the benefits and risks of HRT and offer specific alternatives. A natural menopause is achieved with supplements of vitamins C, B, and E. Calcium with magnesium is also suggested to allay hot flashes and vaginal thinning. They, with Greenwood (1984), offer a comprehensive approach to the many decisions that surround HRT.

Studies on the Effects of HRT

Most of the existing HRT modalities in the 1990s are based on data from the 1980s. It was clear from these studies that post-menopausal estrogen treatment had a well-documented beneficial effect on osteoporosis (Weinstein, 1980). Reduced risk of severe coronary heart disease was also suggested (Stampfer, Willett, Colditz, Rosner, Speizer, & Hennekens, 1985). The use of estrogen to treat menopause symptoms remains controversial because of the contradictory evidence on the role of estrogen in breast cancer development. Exogenous estrogen therapy during the menopause years has usually been prescribed mainly for the relief of symptoms and discomforts of menopause (Rohan and McMichael, 1988). Estrogen replacement therapy was reported beneficial to women in helping them maintain a state of continued well-being. In other words, it alleviates symptoms and discomforts such as vasomotor flushes, headache, backache, poor memory, depression, fatigue, emotional disturbances, and thinning of the genital lining. Perceived risks associated with estrogen intake include endometrial cancer, breast cancer, hypertension, and gallbladder disease (Jenson & Bobak, 1985; Sloane, 1985).

Conversely, Gambrell, Maier, and Sanders (1983), in a prospective study of 5,563 post-menopausal women, produced data that indicated HRT did not increase the risk of breast cancer, and may actually provide some protection. They found that combining progestogen with ERT significantly decreased the risk for developing breast cancer. In still another case-control study by Kaufman, Miller, Rosenberg, Helmrich, Stolley, Schottenfeld, and Shapiro (1984), it was supported that conjugated estrogens did not appear to increase the risk of developing breast cancer. Kaufman, Palmer, deMouzon, Rosenberg, Stolley, Warshauer & Shapiro (1991) found that the overall risk of breast cancer did not increase significantly, even when reported over a 15-year duration. Again, in other similar studies Buring, Hennekens, Lipnick, Willett, Stampfer, Rosner, Peto, and Speizer (1987) and Dupont, Page, Rogers, and Parl (1989) supported the finding that use of exogenous estrogens did not significantly increase the incidence of breast cancer. Rohan and McMichael (1988) and Webster, Wingo, Layde, Lee, Rubin, and Ory (1987) all reported similar findings.

In contrast, several of the older studies demonstrated significant risk of breast cancer associated with ERT. Hoover, Gray, Cole, and MacMahon (1976) did a retrospective cohort study of 1,891 women given conjugated estrogens for menopausal symptoms. They found that, overall, the number of women in their study that developed breast cancer was 30% greater than expected. The risk for those women who had been diagnosed with benign breast disease after beginning ERT was approximately twice that of the general population. Women using higher-dose estrogen tablets in this study were at higher risk for breast cancer.

Studies by Ross, Paganini-Hill, Gerkins, Mack, Arthur, and Henderson (1980) described a conjugated estrogen dose-related risk for breast cancer as early as 1980. Because of the variety of doses and schedules prescribed by physicians, the researchers calculated a single measure of total conjugated estrogen exposure referred to as total milligram accumulated dose (TMD) for each subject. The TMD was based on the sum of the products of the dose of the described pill in milligrams, the number of days each month that the pill was taken, and the total months of consumption for that dose. Low exposure was considered less than 1,500 TMD, and high exposure was 1,500 TMD or more. A TMD of 1,500 is equivalent to approximately three years of taking a daily 1.25 mg. dose of conjugated estrogen. It was shown that a woman who underwent natural menopause by age 50 and took 1.25 mg. of ERT daily for three years was at risk for developing breast cancer by age 75. Subsequently, dosages were lowered and breast cancer risk subsided.

Progesterone

Unlike the role of estrogen intake and the development of breast cancer, the role of progesterone in the protection against breast cancer has been reported by Nachtigall et al. (1979) in their prospective study of the relationships between estrogen replacement therapy and carcinoma. Cardiovascular and metabolic problems were also observed in the study. Nachtigall et al. (1979) found breast cancer risk to be low for a group of estrogen and progesterone treated women. They reported that only 4 out of 84 patients in the control group developed breast cancer.

In 1987, Hunt, Vessey, McPherson, and Coleman conducted a longitudinal surveillance study of mortality and cancer incidence. In this cohort of 4,544 British women receiving hormone replacement therapy, the overall mortality was significantly lower than expected, based on national rates, when progesterone was added.

Sobel (1994) reports on the new gonane progestins that have been used extensively in Europe for over a decade. They have been introduced in the United States only recently. Oral contraceptives using the gonane progestins, containing desogestrel and gestodene, are the most popular prescribed in Europe. The side effects have been minimal with regard to phlebitis and endometrial hyperplasia. However, the data are inconclusive with regard to protection against breast cancer despite the beneficial findings reported by Gambrell et al. (1983) and others listed above, according to Sobel (1994).

Knox reports in *The Boston Globe* (Nov. 18, 1994) of a controlled study of estrogen use by post-menopausal women presented at the Annual Scientific Meeting of the American Heart Association in Dallas, Texas. The study, with funding by the National Institutes of Health, presents strong evidence of the protective effect of estrogen replacement therapy against developing heart disease: in these women, there was at least a 25% reduction. The study was conducted on 875 women over a three-year period.

One of the investigators, Dr. Barrett-Connor, University of California at San Diego, suggests that all post-menopausal women should consult with their physicians regarding HRT if they have had premature surgical menopause, angina, history of heart attack, or other heart disease-related symptoms. She refers to women who do not have these risk factors as the "in between group" who must weigh the risk factors associated with HRT against the benefits. Besides relating the benefits of estrogen, it is strongly suggested that the addition of micronized, as opposed to synthetic, progesterone to protect against uterine cancer did not appear to block the beneficial cardiac effects of the estrogen.

Dr. Trudy Bush, University of Maryland, also one of the researchers working on the study, cautions that a longer and larger study is needed to answer the question of breast cancer risk in women who choose HRT. Her belief is that use of estrogen and progesterone therapy accounts for a very small amount of breast cancer risk. These results bring us closer to solving some of the puzzle pieces. Questions must still be raised about how *low* doses of HRT must be to provide protection, and what remedies are being studied when HRT is contraindicated. Do exercise and diet preclude heart disease anyway in women who are not genetically predisposed? Can the same question be raised about breast cancer?

Hysterectomy

Hysterectomy is another major health issue for midlife women. It is the second most frequently performed surgery in the United States (National Center for Health Statistics, 1988). Doress and Siegal (1994) admonish that women may be submitting themselves to this surgery unnecessarily. They report that only a small percentage (8–12%) of all hysterectomies are performed because of uterine or ovarian cancers. The surgery is usually elective and involves the removal of healthy ovaries. There are projections that 50% of all women will eventually undergo hysterectomy. Doress and Siegal claim that most of the surgeries are performed prior to the menopause, when most of the problems would have subsided anyway. Economic gain for the performing surgeons is one explanation and birth control is another. The surgeries are especially prevalent in women who have health insurance plans that pay for them.

Another interesting factor is that hysterectomy is a regional idiosyncrasy, with higher rates noted in certain cities and states. It is imperative that women become consumers of their own health care in the case of hysterectomy. Hysterectomy should only be performed in the presence of cancer, severe hemorrhaging, large fibroids, advanced pelvic inflammatory disease, severe uterine prolapse, untreatable endometriosis, and other catastrophic conditions that may occur during childbirth (Doress et al., 1994, p. 300).

Hysterectomy surgery is not a minor, risk-free procedure. Most often, it involves general anesthesia, removal of the ovaries and the uterus. Hysterectomy often leads to serious consequences for a pre-menopausal woman. The long-range implications should be carefully considered. It is often suggested that women having the surgery will be better off if they do not choose to bear children at this stage in life. When surgical menopause is performed, the usual prescription that follows is long-term ERT. The previous discussion in this chapter illustrates that hormone therapy may not be a totally benign option because of the still unknown long-term implications of the regimen. Doress and Siegal (1994) offer the most realistic portrayal of the implications of hysterectomy. Their book is an invaluable resource for all women and should be consulted before any major decision is made regarding hysterectomy. It is an especially essential resource for baby-boom women who may eventually face these kinds of decisions.

Bernhard (1992) reported on the consequences of hysterectomy in a sample of 63 women of low socioeconomic class. The women were interviewed prior to the surgery, four weeks post-surgery, three months post-surgery, and two years following the hysterectomy. Prior to the surgery, most of the women had positive feelings that persisted for at least three months with 14% of the women having negative feelings and 49% sharing mixed feelings. Most of the women had received mixed messages about the possible effects of hysterectomy. Over half of the women had positive information from their physicians and negative information from friends and family. When the same women were surveyed two years later, more than half of the women reported negative feelings. Symptoms such as depression, irritability, nervousness, and blue spells were commonly reported and attributed to their hysterectomies. Hot flashes and night sweats were also present in some of the women. It was concluded by Bernhard that the long-term effects of hysterectomy are not well understood and that women in all socioeconomic groups should be studied and supported before and after they undergo hysterectomy.

Plastic Surgery

The concept of elective plastic surgery has affected millions of women in the middle years. Some have raised the notion that women who submit to plastic surgery are denying the aging process and have low self-esteem (Sheehy, 1991). Judgments such as these are unwarranted. Many women who choose plastic surgery may not lack in self-esteem, but rather make choices that are best for them. Some women have a genetic disposition to excessive wrinkling, or may have been born with a disfiguring bone structure. Others may feel they do not look their best because of the bags under the eyes and on their upper lids that interfere with their eyesight. They may have any number of other reasons to make an informed choice for cosmetic plastic surgery. On the other hand, careful weighing of the reasons for the surgery and possible consequences of the plastic surgery performed by unqualified surgeons may prevent disfigurement and a life of pain.

The issue of breast reconstruction following mastectomy, or for the purpose of breast augmentation, has received a great deal of publicity in recent years. In April 1994, a settlement of over $4 billion was announced in a class action suit against the manufacturer of silicone implants (Dow-Corning Corporation) and its suppliers. The lawsuit originated from the United States District Court for the northern district of Alabama. One of the lawsuits filed in the state of Alabama has been certified as a class action for women who have had, or within the next thirty years will develop any one of several diseases as a result of silicone or silicone-encased saline breast implants. The projected net settlements are expected to range from between $105,000 to $1,400,000 depending on the disease, severity, and the claimants' age. The covered diseases are:

1. Systemic and Localized Sclerosis or Scleroderma
2. Systemic Lupus Erythematosus

3. Atypical Neurological Disease Syndrome
4. Connective Tissue Disease
5. Polymyositis
6. Dermatomyositis
7. Atypical Connective Disease
8. Atypical Rheumatic Syndrome
9. Nonspecific Autoimmune Condition
10. Sjogren's Syndrome

(United States District Court, Northern District of Alabama v. Dow-Corning Corporation, Lindsey et al., 1994).

The list of complications that will be compensated for is grim. This is certainly an issue for thousands of midlife women in this country. Many women whose health was devastated had innocently chosen either to restore their bodies following mastectomy or to augment their breasts for whatever personal reason. Instead, they discover silicone leaking and infiltrating tissues throughout their bodies, leaving them with autoimmune diseases such as those mentioned above.

Pregnancy

Lately, it has been reported in the popular press that older, nonovulating women are being impregnated with donor eggs fertilized with sperm from their partners. In one instance, a 63-year-old woman gave birth to a healthy child that was conceived through the efforts of a fertility specialist who has assisted 47 women over the age of 50 to bear children in this manner (Carlson, 1994). This poses an ethical dilemma for some. Others are questioning why no criticism is raised when men in midlife or older become fathers. Is the female body a political object as some have claimed or is this a legitimate ethical argument against older women giving birth? Are women putting their own health at risk to fulfill unrealistic child-rearing expectations? There are many unanswered questions concerning the prospect of post-menopause women delivering artificially conceived children. Certainly this is an issue that will continue to confront baby-boom midlife women who have delayed childbearing and still wish to bear children at a later stage in their lives.

Stress and Depression

Mythically, and as result of Freudian beliefs, midlife women have been characterized as depressed and maladapted. Recent studies have found the opposite to be true. As early as 1979, Rubin reported that the majority of midlife women were geared up for a life of their own and were joyful at having their children leave home. Her report discounts the empty nest syndrome, when all mothers are characterized as being so distraught that they go into deep depression when their children leave. However, it is sometimes difficult to convince older children that their mothers are enjoying their newfound freedom and life satisfaction with their children out of the house. For a small majority of women who have lived vicariously through their husbands and children and who have been unable to adapt to life without children, stress and depression may indeed be present.

When women in midlife do report stress, it is often associated with a desire to remain young within the sociocultural expectations for youth and vigor (Barbee, 1989). However, when midlife women participate in exercise, work outside the home, and other adaptive lifestyle practices, they report significantly less depression and psychological distress than those women who do not remain active (Norvell, Martin, & Salamon, 1991).

Costello (1991) conducted a study of 541 midlife women regarding predictors of mental and physical health. It was reported that women who were married, had children, worked outside the home, and had a college education were more than twice as happy as women who stayed at home and did not pursue a college education or any kind of advanced preparation. It appears that in her study a high level of education and working outside the home led to a higher sense of life satisfaction and a lower rate of depression. Paid employment, regardless of educational level, was also associated with significantly low rates of depression. Living a productive life, as a contributing member of society, filled with an abundance of rewarding activities, can be predictive of good mental health and attitude.

Marriage

Rubin (1983) postulates that older men who become fathers, often with a younger partner, are merely validating their lives. She claims that some of these men have lived their lives going off to work each day without sharing the various developmental stages experienced by their own offspring. Suddenly, their children are grown and their once young and beautiful wives are now older and may be perceived by some husbands as haggard and wrinkled. It is at this time, Rubin believes, that a midlife crisis occurs and a relationship with a younger woman, and sometimes a new family, emerges.

Midlife women, on the other hand, have witnessed each childhood stage, and are most generally prepared when their last child grows up and leaves home. Midlife crisis is not as obvious for these women, whose midlife transition consists of simply looking at life's limits and deciding on a new direction. If their marriage is intact at this juncture, it must be renegotiated in order for it to survive, Rubin claims. This is the phase in life when children no longer require parenting and the child-rearing bond between the marriage partners is weakened. During this stage, the midlife marriage is most vulnerable. A concerted effort is necessary for the marriage partners to develop new interests together that will help to cement their relationship.

Scharf (1987) deals with a contemporary overview of marriage and the changes that occur over time. Five couples were analyzed using case study methodology as they dealt with the cyclical tasks confronting all married couples. An attempt is made to carefully describe the architecture in each of the prototype marriages and its effect on either eventual divorce or reconciliation. There is an in-depth discussion of human sexuality with strategies for coming to terms with dysfunctional behaviors in marriage. Inability to achieve sexual harmony because of lack of knowledge about sexuality is often seen as a major cause of marital misunderstanding. A basic understanding of the causes of conflict within marriage is essential. For individuals who are seeking their way through midlife within the marriage structure, Scharf presents a comprehensive guide.

Batteson (1990) advises us that, far from the accepted stereotypes, marriage and child-rearing are not alternatives to achieving personal success and self-actualization. The women she describes have created their own growth environments outside of the home, and within the tasks of homemaking and caregiving. These women have been creative in all aspects of their self-fulfillment within the parameters of marriage and other long-lasting relationships. She speaks for all women when she admonishes that there is no such thing as a superwoman. She advises that, as we get older, it is important to conserve our energy by avoiding fatigue, jet lag, and stress. Caring for our bodies is essential so that we will have more to offer. It appears that Batteson is teaching us that we must remain interesting to others and excited about life so that others will seek our company and so that we too will feel fulfilled and happy.

Widowhood

Surprisingly, in my own research of midlife, women who have become widows report that they experience relatively high life satisfaction and low anxiety. Contrary to societal notions about stress and depression in older widows, many are leading complete lives filled with family, career, and outside interests (Jacobson, 1993). Maxwell (1988) also found that widows who were educated, worked outside the home, and were less traditional appeared to experience widowhood in an adaptive manner. The findings may hold given that the widows are in good health, financially secure, and relatively young (Doress & Siegal, 1994). The implication is that women who continue to live their lives to the fullest following a major loss may adapt if they remain connected to life and others. This is a relevant finding that may be of interest when baby-boom women find themselves contemplating life without a spouse or significant other.

Kelly (1991) discusses widowhood in the context of the elderly individual who has never developed or self-actualized, previously described as living vicariously through one's family. This type of individual has never become independent. In this situation, the elderly individual has great difficulty coping with bereavement, life without her lifelong partner, and the lifestyle they enjoyed as a couple. Not only has the grieving widow lost her husband, but also the friends they enjoyed together. Kelly also relates that the inability to maintain her home alone is another loss that must be faced and is a problem for the newly widowed older individual.

Kelly's work can help us to understand that, in order to avoid these pitfalls, one must prepare for the eventuality of widowhood by developing a sense of oneself early in life. The grieving process may not be as painful an event for contemporary midlife women because of their socialization and options for self-fulfillment and independence within the marital framework. Doress and Siegal (1994) remind us that widowhood is an inevitable experience that will affect most married women simply because most women outlive men in our society. The average age for widowhood is 65 and healthy women generally live another 18 years after a husband's passing (p. 138).

It is essential to recognize that it is important to take time to grieve in order to come to terms with widowhood. For those women who find themselves widowed, the ensuing tasks involve finding one's identity and developing outside interests. Doress and Siegal (1994) offer numerous interventions for creating a new life as well as suggestions for seeking support systems in the community.

Divorce

The escalating rate of divorce in midlife continues to be an issue for midlife women who must adjust to loss of important social relationships. According to Norton and Miller (1992), the baby-boom generation is likely to have the highest rates of divorce of any other cohort before them. Ever since the 1960s the change in the general patterns of first marriage, divorce, and remarriage have profoundly changed the patterns of American family life. It was during this time that the rates of first marriage began to fall, signaling an era of putting off marriage and family in order for women to pursue careers and educational opportunities. Divorce rates began to rise as well in the 1960s. Roughly 50% of all marriages between the 1960s and the 1980s ended in divorce. The rates for the 1990s remain high as well. Remarriage rates began to rise initially in the 1960s and then declined. The marriage rate trends have been more difficult to predict with later marriage persisting and many individuals choosing to remain single.

Norton and Miller (1992) report on an emerging dichotomy between black and white women. Fewer black women, less than three out of four, will ever marry and those who do choose marriage will do so later in life, this compared to nine out of ten white women who will eventually marry. Hispanic women, they report, generally follow in the same marriage patterns as white women. According to Norton and Miller (1992), a high divorce rate equates with a large pool of eligible remarriage partners. More than four out of ten marriages presently reflect multiple prior marriages. Norton and Miller project a tendency for older divorced women to remain single in the 1990s.

Predictors of divorce are marrying young, conceiving or bearing children prior to marriage, and leaving either high school or college before graduation in order to marry. Divorce has increased the numbers of single-parent families. It is usually the mother who is left to raise the children, although there is a pattern of male single-parent families emerging (Norton & Miller, 1992). In addition to dealing with the usual sandwich generation issues of coping with adolescent children and elderly parents simultaneously, midlife divorcees must also deal with shrinking remarriage prospects if they are over 50. Unless these women are left with an extraordinarily large divorce settlement, work and career become important considerations (Bogolub, 1991). Rubin (1979) spoke of divorced women going from rich to poor, and from companionship to loneliness. Most women, however, adjust to their new lives following the initial shock of divorce. Friendships also take a new direction for the newly divorced who are often seen as a threat to their married friends. For older midlife women, this adjustment may be more difficult. The issue of preretirement planning is also imperative for the midlife woman in order to assure a secure lifestyle in her golden years (Dennis, 1984).

Remarriage implies reconstituted and blended families, and the readjustment that must be accomplished if the subsequent marriage is to succeed. Re-divorce occurs sooner than the first divorce and is a growing phenomenon that is projected to increase. Predictions for the future suggest that the tendency toward later marriage will continue, there will be more single-parent families with never married mothers, the divorce rate will decrease with four out of ten marriages ending in divorce and rates of remarriage will also decrease (Norton & Miller, 1992).

Krantzler (1981) reported that, although the institution of marriage is still alive and well, serial marriages are becoming a recognized entity. The notion of family solidarity still exists, but in a revised form of blended families and large family networks of stepparents and grandparents.

Knox (1977) also noted that the institution of marriage in the United States and in other developed parts of the world has changed drastically in recent years. Although it is reported that most divorces occur in the first years of marriage, a sharp increase has been noted during the middle years.

Russianoff (1981) offered a philosophical explanation for the increasing divorce rates. She equated the increasing rates to the women's movement and applauded women's freedom to make choices toward personal growth and fulfillment that are now acceptable in today's society. On the downside, she describes the many women who have forgone education and careers and have found themselves in severe economic straits following divorce. The resulting turmoil in a divorced woman's life can lead to midlife crisis. Interventions such as reentry programs offered at many colleges and universities are essential for survival in contemporary society. It is relevant for both divorced and widowed women who find themselves alone to seek self-help approaches. Difficult issues such as rebuilding a new life, meeting new people, managing finances, finding a job, and dealing with family members are described by McConnell and Anderson (1978).

Aburdene and Naisbitt (1992) share some hopeful reflections for the children of the earliest baby boomers who may have experienced the highest divorce rates in history firsthand. They predict that this generation of children, now young adults, will work hard to achieve success in marriage because of the pain that they endured growing up in divorced families with either a single-parent or a blended family.

Parenting Grown Children

Some women have difficulty letting go of their grown children. This is true in the case of many pre-baby-boom midlife women who have never worked outside the home and who have lived vicariously through their children. I call these women *Vicarious Livers* because they have never lived a life of their own, separate from their families. This is not to downgrade motherhood and all of its sacrifices and joys, but, unless these women begin to find their own way and self-actualize, the relationship with their grown children may become tenuous. For these women, allowing their children to make their own decisions without interference must be achieved or disharmony will occur.

Doress and Siegal (1994) echo these observations and expound on the aspect of becoming a mother-in-law. The key here is to stop short of having a shredded tongue by respecting your married children, and allowing them the right to make decisions without your input. A fresh approach must be developed between midlife mothers whose children have left the nest (Rubin, 1979). It is imperative that friendship and respect for the young adult's newfound independence be cultivated. It often presents a delicate balance between being available for advice, but never offering any.

Rubin (1979) has disproved the myth of the empty nest, except in the case of the woman who lives through her family, and notes that children become less dependent on their parents as they mature. However, there is an emerging pattern of the revolving door syndrome, when adult children return home following divorce or for financial reasons. McKinlay (1986) describes this as a potential source of conflict for the midlife mother. This phenomenon may not be relevant for the baby-boom woman who has either delayed childbearing, had a small family, or chosen not to have children at all.

Caring for Aging Parents

For midlife baby-boom women, the idea of caring for aging parents also presents a new dimension. This is the first generation that has experienced the results of increased longevity. Most elderly parents choose to remain independent for as long as possible. It should be recognized that a large percentage of elders continue to work well after their 65th birthdays (Silverstone & Hyman, 1982).

However, for those elders who need a caregiving daughter or daughter-in-law to assist them, the problems can become overwhelming. Caregiving experiences are different for daughters than they are for wives and nonparticipating siblings, who are often a potential source of additional stress. Patterns of caregiving are changing because many working women are also expected to perform numerous family roles (Silverstone & Hyman, 1982).

Slowly, the stigma of placing an infirm or demented parent into a nursing home is eroding. Families often seek nursing home placements simply to relieve themselves of the overwhelming stress encountered when caring for an elderly parent. Despite the immediate relief when a parent is placed in a nursing home, other burdens are encountered as caregiving children are expected to participate in emotionally draining routine visits. Feelings of inadequacy, guilt, and grief at the loss of the cognitive abilities of the infirm parent may precipitate a sense of loss and distress (Pallett, 1990). Fortunately, there are many resources available to assist adult children with aging parents. However, it should be noted that long-term care is not covered in any of the existing government programs. It is not very likely that this will change in the future because of the high costs of maintaining an elderly person in a nursing home.

The government has provided a safety umbrella for the elder population with the medicare and social security programs, but these programs are fraught with controversy because of their escalating costs. This is in part a result of the growing elder population at 31 million Americans over 65 in 1990. This population is projected to grow to 52 million by 2020 and 68 million by 2040. It is projected that when the baby-boom generation enters the ranks of old age, the system may become bankrupt. Many solutions to the problem are being considered by Congress. Some of the solutions suggested to control the rising costs of medicare may include living wills that prohibit extensive and futile life-support measures in the last stages of life. Increasing the tax on social security benefits for elders who report a certain level of income is presently under consideration by some in Congress to compensate for these escalating costs (Lee & Estes, 1994).

Grandparenting

Grandparenting in midlife is another dimension of the midlife experience. Many baby boomers are experiencing this role in a variety of ways. For some, the parenting role is reassumed. This may be the case when unwed mothers are not capable or able to raise their own children. Other instances may occur that prevent young parents from caring for their own children.

Some very nontraditional grandmothers are in vogue because of the changing roles of women during the past thirty years. These grandmothers are often still very active in the work force as well as in their personal lives. They are reported to being involved in selling real estate, flying planes, creating businesses, writing best-selling novels, acting, playing at various types of sports. Most often, they are unavailable to baby-sit for their grandchildren, or even see them on a regular basis. Frequently, because of our mobile society, midlife grandmothers may be thousands of miles away from their grandchildren and may see them rarely on special occasions or vacations (Wyse, 1989).

In most instances, a special relationship between grandchildren and grandmothers is enjoyed. Some of the so-called terrible things children do may go unnoticed as grandmothers become captivated by the brilliant things their grandchildren are accomplishing. This can be a very rewarding relationship (Wyse, 1989). These special relationships may continue throughout a child's life and offer a pleasurable dimension for both child and grandmother. This special relationship may also reinforce self-esteem in a child.

Baby-boom grandmothers may experience this dimension of becoming a grandparent later in life because they have often delayed childbearing. When they do become grandparents, they will certainly offer their own unique dimension to grandparenting. Again Doress and Siegal (1994) interject that grandparenting is closely associated with being a mother-in-law. They suggest that we become peers to our daughters and daughters-in-law in relating to each other as mothers. Nevertheless, it is imperative that we recognize the autonomy of our children and our in-laws and we must allow them to make their own child-rearing decisions without our advice unless of course it is solicited.

Summary

This chapter illustrates the numerous health and psychological challenges that face women in midlife. The overriding message is that women should be informed of the risk factors for disease and the treatment options set before them. Seeking independent second opinions when necessary is essential. The baby-boom generation of midlife women is probably the most well informed of any that preceded them, and they will demand answers and solutions for their own health and psychological questions.

In the ensuing chapter, I will describe my research on 962 midlife women. The results of the study illustrated that age did not appear to be a factor in determining life satisfaction and high levels of anxiety. Those factors that influence anxiety and life satisfaction will also be discussed. Similarities appear to exist between the baby-boom midlife women and their older cohorts in midlife. Clearly, a new form of traditionalism is emerging as the baby-boom women adapt to midlife.

References

Aburdene, P., & Naisbitt, J. (1992). *Megatrends for women.* New York: Fawcett Columbine.

Adami, H.O., Bergstrom, R., & Sparen, P. (1993). Increasing cancer risk in younger birth cohorts in Sweden. *Lancet, 341,* 773–777.

American Cancer Society. (1994). *Cancer facts and figures.* Atlanta: American Cancer Society.

American Heart Association. (1993). 1993 Heart and stroke facts statistics. Dallas, TX: National Center.

Anderson, I., Aspergren, K., Janzon, L., Landberg, T., Lindholm, K., Linnell, F., Ljungberg, O., Ranstam, J., & Sigfusson, B. (1988). Mammographic screening and mortality from breast cancer: The Malmo mammographic screening trial. *British Medical Journal, 297,* 943–948.

Ayanian, J.Z., & Epstein, A.M. (1991). Differences in the use of procedures between women and men hospitalized for coronary heart disease. *New England Journal of Medicine, 325*(4), 221–225.

Banner, L.W. (1992). *In full flower.* New York: Vintage Books.

Barbee, E.L. (1989). Worries, aging, and desires to be younger in a sample of American middle-aged women. *Medical Anthropology, 12*(1), 117–129.

Batteson, M.C. (1990). *Composing a life.* New York: Plume Books: The Atlantic Monthly Press.

Bergkvist, L., Adami, H., Persson, I., Hoover, R., & Schairer, L. (1989). The risk of breast cancer after estrogen & estrogen-progestogen replacement. *New England Journal of Medicine, 321,* 293–297.

Bernhard, L.A. (1992). Consequences of hysterectomy in the lives of women. *Health Care for Women International, 13,* 281–291.

Bogolub, E.B. (1991). Women and midlife divorce: Some practice issues. *Social Work, 36*(5), 428–433.

Boring, C.C., Squires, T.S., & Tong, T. (1992). *Cancer statistics 1992.* Atlanta: American Cancer Society, Inc.

Boston Women's Health Collective (1992). *The new our bodies ourselves.* New York: Simon & Schuster.

Brinton, L.A., Hoover, R., & Fraumeni, J.F. (1983). Epidemiology of minimal breast cancer. *Journal of the American Medical Association, 289,* 483–487.

Buring, J.E., Hennekens, C.H., Lipnick, R.J., Willett, W., Stampfer, M.J., Rosner, B., Peto, R., & Speizer, F. (1987). A prospective cohort study of postmenopausal hormone use & risk of breast cancer in US women. *American Journal of Epidemiology, 125,* 939–947.

Bush, T.L., & Helzlouer, K.J. (1993). Tamoxifen for the primary prevention of breast cancer: A review and critique on the concept and trial. *Epidemiologic Reviews, The Johns Hopkins University School of Hygiene and Public Health, 15*(1), 233–243.

Campbell, S., & Whitehead, M. (1977). Estrogen therapy and menopausal syndrome. *Clinics in Obstetrics and Gynecology, 4*(1), 31–47.

Carlson, M. (January 10, 1994). Old enough to be your mother. *Time,* 41.

Carter, C.L., Jones, D.Y., Schatzkin, A., & Brinton, L.A. (1989). A prospective study of reproductive, familial, and socioeconomic risk factors for breast cancer using NHANES 1 data. *Public Health Reports, 104*(1), 45–50.

Colditz, G.A., Stampfer, M.J., Willett, W.C., Hennekens, C.H., Rosner, B., & Speizer, F.E. (1990). A prospective study of estrogen replacement therapy and risk of breast cancer in postmenopausal women. *Journal of the American Medical Association, 264,* 2648–2653.

Costello, E.J. (1991). Married with children: Predictors of mental and physical health in middle-aged women. *Psychiatry, 54*(3), 292–305.

Cotton, P. (1992). Women's health initiative leads the way as research begins to fill gender gaps. *Journal of the American Medical Association, 267,* 469–470, 473.

Davis, D.L., Dinse, G.E., & Hoel, D.G. (February 9, 1994). Decreasing cardiovascular disease and increasing cancer among whites in the United States from 1973 through 1987. *Journal of the American Medical Association, 271*(6), 431–437.

Dennis, H. (1984). *Retirement preparation.* Lexington, MA: D.C. Heath and Company.

Doress, P.B., & Siegal, D.S. (1994). *Ourselves growing older.* In cooperation with the Boston Women's Health Collective. New York: Simon and Schuster.

Dupont, W.D., Page, D.L., Rogers, L.W., & Parl, F.F. (1989). Influence of exogenous estrogens, proliferative breast disease & other variables on breast cancer risk. *Cancer, 63,* 948–957.

Erikson, E.H. (1950). *Childhood and society.* New York: W.W. Norton.

Felson, D.T., Zhang, Y., Hannan, M.T., Kiel, D.P., Wilson, P.W., & Anderson, J.J. (October 14, 1993). The effect of postmenopausal therapy on bone density in elderly women. *New England Journal of Medicine, 329*(16), 1141–1146.

Friend, S.H. (March 29, 1994). *Breast cancer genetic research update.* Seminar: The Center for Cancer Risk Analysis, Massachusetts General Hospital Cancer Center.

Fugh-Berman, A., & Epstein, S. (November 7, 1992). Tamoxifen: Disease prevention or disease substitution? *Lancet, 340,* 1143–1144.

Gambrell, R.D., Maier, R.C., & Sanders, B.I. (1983). Decreased incidence of breast cancer in postmenopausal estrogen users. *Obstetrics & Gynecology, 62,* 435–443.

Gambrell, R.D., Jr. (1987). Hormone replacement therapy and breast cancer. *Maturitas, 9,* 123–133.

Graham, S. (1987). Alcohol and breast cancer: *New England Journal of Medicine, 295,* 401–405.

Greenwood, S. (1984). *Menopause naturally.* San Francisco: Volcano Press.

Hoover. R., Gray L. A., Cole, P., MacMahon, B. (1976). Menopausal estrogens and breast cancer. *New England Journal of Medicine, 295,* 401–405.

Hulka, C.A. (March 29, 1994). *New imaging* techniques seminar: The Center for Cancer Risk Analysis, Massachusetts General Hospital Cancer Center.

Hunt, K., Vessey, M., McPherson, K., & Coleman, M. (1987). Long-term surveillance of mortality and cancer incidence in women receiving hormone replacement therapy. *British Journal of Obstetrics and Gynecology, 94,* 620–635.

Jacobson, J.M. (1993). Midlife baby-boom women compared to their older counterparts in midlife. *Health Care for Women International, (14),* 427–436.

Jacobson, J.M. (1995). Risk factors for breast cancer. Preliminary findings. Unpublished.

Jenson, M., & Bobak, I. (1985). *Maternity and gynecologic care.* 3rd ed. St. Louis: The C.V. Mosby Company.

Kaufman, D.W., Miller, D.R., Rosenberg, L., Helmrich, S.P., Stolley, P., Schottenfeld, D., & Shapiro, S. (1984). Non-contraceptive estrogen use and the risk of breast cancer. *Journal of the American Medical Association, 252,* 63–67.

Kaufman, D.W., Palmer, J.R., deMouzon, J., Rosenberg, L., Stolley, P.D., Worshauer, M.E., & Shapiro, S. (1991). Estrogen replacement therapy and the risk of breast cancer: Results from the case-control surveillance study. *American Journal of Epidemiology, 134*(12), 1375–1385.

Kelly, B. (1991). Emily: A study of grief and bereavement. *Health Care for Women International, 12,* 137–147.

Kirkman-Liff, B., & Kronenfeld, J.J. (1992). Access to cancer screening services for women. *American Journal of Public Health, 82*(5), 733–735.

Knox, A.B. (1977). *Adult learning and development.* San Francisco: Jossey-Bass Publishers.

Knox, R.A. (1994, November 18). Estrogen role in cutting heart risk confirmed. *The Boston Globe,* pp. 1, 14.

Korenman, S.G. (1980). Estrogen window hypothesis of the etiology of breast cancer. *Lancet, 2,* 700–701.

Krantzler, M. (1981). *Creative marriage.* New York: Human Science Press.

Lee, P.R., & Estes, C.L. (1994). *The nation's health.* Boston: Jones & Bartlett Publishers.

Liff, J.M., Sung, J.F.C., Chow, W., Greenberg, R.S., & Flanders, W.D. (1991). Does increased detection account for the rising incidence of breast cancer? *American Journal of Public Health, 81,* 462–465.

Lipnick, R., Speizer, F.E., Bain, C., Willett, W., Rosner, B., Stampfer, M.J., Belanger, C., & Hennekens, C.H. (1984). A case-control study of risk indicators among women with postmenopausal and early postmenopausal breast cancer. *Cancer, 31,* 1020–1024.

Lubin, F., Ruder, A.M., Wax, Y., Modan, B. (1985). Overweight and changes in weight throughout adult life in breast cancer etiology. *American Journal of Epidemiology, 122,* 579–588.

Maxwell, E.K. (1988). Status differences in cohorts of aging women. *Health Care for Women International, 9,* 83–91.

McConnell, A., & Anderson, B. (1978). *Single after 50.* New York: McGraw-Hill.

McElmurry, B.J., & Parker, R.S. (1993). *Annual review of women's health.* New York: National League for Nursing Press Pub. No. 19-2546.

McKinlay, J., & McKinlay, S. (1986). *Women and their health in Massachusetts.* Cambridge, MA: Cambridge Research Center.

Miller, D.R., Rosenberg, L., Kaufman, D.W., Schottenfeld, D., Stolley, P.D., &

Shapiro, S. (1986). Breast cancer risk in relation to early oral contraceptive use. *Obstetrics & Gynecology, 68,* 863–868.

Mills, P.K., Beeson, W.L., Phillips, R.L., & Fraser, G.E. (August, 1989). Dietary habits and breast cancer incidence among Seventh-day Adventists. *Cancer.* 582–590.

Nachtigall, L.E., Nachtigall, R.H., Nachtigall, R.D., & Beckman, E.M. (1979). Estrogen replacement therapy II: A prospective study in the relationship to carcinoma and cardiovascular and metabolic problems. *Obstetrics & Gynecology, 54*(1), 74–49.

National Cancer Institute. (September 1992). *Cancer statistics review 1973-1989.*

National Center for Health Statistics, Hospital Care Statistics Branch. (1988). *Advance data from vital and health statistics.* DHHS Pub. No. (PHS) 88–1250. Hyattsville, MD: U.S. Public Health Service.

Norton, A.J. & Miller, L.F. (1992). Marriage, divorce, and remarriage in the 1990s. Washington, D.C.: U.S. Bureau of the Census. U.S. Government Printing Office, 1–21.

Norvell, N., Martin, D., & Salamon, A. (1991). Psychological and physiological benefits of passive and aerobic exercise. *Journal of Nervous and Mental Disease, 179*(9), 573–574.

Olsson, H., Ranstam, J., Baldetorp, B., Ewers, S., Ferno, M., Killander, D., & Sigurdsson, H. (1991). Proliferation and DNA in malignant breast tumors in relation to early oral contraceptive use and early abortions. *Cancer, 67,* 1285–1290.

Osteen, R.T., Connolly, J.L., Costanza, M.E., Harris, J.R., Henderson, I.C., & McKenney, S. (1990). Cancer of the breast. *Cancer Manual.* Boston: The American Cancer Society, 171–190.

Ottman, R., King, M.C., Pike, C., & Henderson, B.E. (1983). Practical guide for estimating risk for familial breast cancer. *Lancet, 3,* 556–558.

Pallett, P.J. (1990). A conceptual framework for studying family caregiver burden in Alzheimer's type dementia. *Image, 22*(1), 52–57.

Rennie, S. (January/February, 1993). Dietary fat and breast cancer issue is not settled. *The National Women's Health Network News,* 5.

Rohan, T.E., & McMichael, A.J. (1988). Non-contraceptive exogenous estrogen therapy and breast cancer. *Medical Journal of Australia, 148,* 217–221.

Romieir, I., Oberlin, J.A., & Colditz, G. (1990). Oral contraceptives and breast cancer. Review and meta-analysis. *Cancer, 66,* 2253–2263.

Roseman, D.L., Straus, A.K., & Shorey, W. (1990). A positive family history of breast cancer. Does its effect diminish with age? *Archives of Internal Medicine, 150,* 191–194.

Rosenberg, L. (1993). Hormone replacement therapy: The need for reconsideration. *American Journal of Public Health, 83*(12), 1670–1672.

Ross, R.K., Paganini-Hill, A., Gerkins, V. R., Mack, T. M., Arthur, M., & Henderson, B.E. (1980). A case-control study of menopausal estrogen therapy and breast cancer. *Journal of the American Medical Association, 243,* 1635–1639.

Rubin, L. (1979). *Women of a certain age.* New York: Harper & Row.

Rubin, L. (1983). *Intimate strangers.* New York: Harper & Row.

Russianoff, P. (1981). *Women in crisis.* New York: Human Science Press.

Sattin, R.W., Rubin, G.L., & Webster, L.A. (1985). Family history and the risk of breast cancer. *Journal of the American Medical Association, 253,* 1908–1913.

Scharf, M. (1987). *Intimate partners.* New York: Random House.

Schatzkin, A., Jones, D.Y., Hoover, R.N., Taylor, P.R., Brinton, L.A., Zeigler, R.G., Harvey, E.B., Carter, C.L., Licitra, L.M., Dufour, M.C., & Larson, D. B. (1987). Alcohol consumption and breast cancer in the epidemiologic follow-up study of the first national health and nutrition examination survey. *New England Journal of Medicine, 316,* 1169–1173.

Schlesselman, J.J., Stadel, B.V., Murray, P., & Lai, S. (1988). Breast cancer in relation to early use of oral contraceptives. *Journal of the American Medical Association, 259,* 1828–1883.

Sheehy, G. (1993). *The silent passage.* New York: Pocket Books.

Silverstone, B., & Hyman, H.K. (1982). *You and your aging parent.* New York: Pantheon Books.

Sloane, E. (1985). *Biology of women. 2nd ed.* New York: John Wiley & Sons.

Sobel, N.B. (1994, June). Progestins in preventive hormone therapy. *Obstetrics and Gynecology Clinics of North America, 21*(2), 299–319.

Stampfer, M.J., Willett, W.C., Colditz, G.A., Rosner, B., Speizer, F.E., & Hennekens, C.H. (1985). A prospective study of postmenopausal estrogen treatment and coronary heart disease. *New England Journal of Medicine, 313,* 1044–1049.

Steinberg, K.A., Thacker, S.B., Smith, S.J., Stroup, D.F., Zack, M.M., Flanders, W.D., & Berkleman, R.L. (1991). A meta-analysis of the effect of estrogen replacement therapy on risk of breast cancer. *Journal of the American Medical Association, 264*(15), 1985–1990.

The Boston Women's Health Collective. (1992). *The new our bodies ourselves.* New York: Simon & Schuster, Inc.

United States District Court, Northern District of Alabama (1994) Lindsey et al. vs. Dow-Corning, et al. In re: *Silicone Gel Breast Implant Products Liability.* Master File No. CV, 92 P 100000S.

Vessey, M.P., Doll, R., Jones, K., McPherson, K., & Yeates, D. (1979). An epidemiological study of oral contraceptives and breast cancer. *British Medical Journal, 1,* 1755–1758.

Webster, H., Wingo, P.A., Layde, P.M., Lee, N.C., Rubin, G., & Ory, H.W. (1987). The risk of breast cancer in postmenopausal women who have used estrogen replacement therapy. *Journal of the American Medical Association, 257,* 209–215.

Weinstein, M.C. (1980). Estrogen use in postmenopausal women—costs, risks, benefits. *New England Journal of Medicine, 305,* 308–316.

Willett, W., & Hunter, D.J. (1993). Diet and breast cancer. *Contemporary Nutrition, 18*(3,4), 1–4.

Willett, W.C., Stampfer, M.J., Colditz, G.A., Rosner, B.A., Hennekens, C.H., & Speizer, F.E. (1987). Moderate alcohol consumption and the risk of breast cancer. *New England Journal of Medicine, 313,* 1174–1180.

Willett, W.C., Stampfer, M.J., Colditz, G.A., Rosner, B.A., Hennekens, C.H., & Speizer, F.E. (1987). Dietary fat and the risk of breast cancer. *New England Journal of Medicine, 316,* 22–28.

Williams, B.K., and Knight, S.M. (1994). *Healthy for life: Wellness and the art of living.* Pacific Grove, CA: Brooks Cole Publishing Company.

Wynder, E.L., Rose, D.P., & Cohen, L.A. (1986). Diet and breast cancer in causation and therapy. *Cancer, 58,* 1804–1813.

Wyse, L. (1989). *Funny you don't look like a grandmother.* New York: Crown Publishers, Inc.

Zhang, J., Feldblum, P.J., & Fortney, J.A. (1992). Moderate physical activity and bone marrow density among perimenopausal women. *American Journal of Public Health, 82*(5), 736–738.

Chapter 4

Midlife Baby-Boom Women Compared
to Their Older Counterparts in Midlife

In this chapter, my research study involving nearly 1,000 midlife women who were graduates of a large private university in southern California is presented. The women in the study were born between 1933 and 1953, encompassing the baby-boom generation as well as the midlife women who preceded them. The study was undertaken for the purpose of gaining an increased understanding of the baby-boom cohort of midlife women as compared to their older counterparts in midlife. It was important to explore whether the baby-boom midlife women, born after January 1, 1946, were different from or similar to those midlife women who preceded them. It was anticipated that because there are no cultural norms to describe the contemporary midlife experience, an enhanced understanding of this developmental stage would be gained through my study. Societal changes have rendered the experience of contemporary baby-boom midlife women as different from those who preceded them.

Baby boomers are seeking knowledge as they make the passage into the middle years. The information available to them is often fraught with myths surrounding midlife women. These myths have been perpetuated because of a dearth of empirical study on women in this life stage. The reader will recall that previous studies of midlife women reflected mainly on dysfunctional women and were based on Freudian theory. The early midlife studies were conducted by male researchers with male subjects, and were biased because they considered women deviant if they differed from the men in the studies (Duffy, 1985). Gilligan (1982) contends that eminent male researchers such as Piaget, Kohlberg, Erikson, Levinson, and Valliant either left female subjects out of their studies of developmental theory entirely, or concluded that feminine behavior was deviant according to male behavioral norms. Contemporary feminist writers deny that women are highly anxious and show deviant behavior (Chodorow, 1978; Keohane, Rosaldo, & Gelpi, 1981). Thankfully, modern societal changes, and the advent of the baby-boom generation into midlife, has caused the slow erosion of some of the myths and misconceptions that abound.

One of the questions posed in the study was to determine how these changes have impinged upon the newest generation of midlife women. Measures of life satisfaction and anxiety were applied to all of the women in the study. Comparisons between the baby boomers and their older cohorts were made to determine whether the younger cohort was experiencing increased stress because of the diverse roles thrust upon them.

Background

Both Kessler-Harris (1982) and Jones (1981) describe the baby-boom generation as one that enjoyed the privilege of affluence and opportunities not available to their older counterparts during the time that they were socialized. Along with these opportunities and newfound freedom, however, came the drug culture and the sexual revolution. These children of the sixties were different and became more liberal than any that had ever preceded them. They are the largest cohort that this country has ever known. Jones (1981) recalled that they affected and changed every institution that they came into contact with. They were known as the anti-establishment generation and they disavowed many of the values espoused by their parents and grandparents, including patriotism and allegiance to their country. This generation dared to disagree with their government and protested against its policies during the Vietnam era.

Pre-Baby-Boom Midlife Women

On the other hand, pre-baby-boom midlife women, now in their late 40s and 50s, were socialized under an entirely different set of circumstances. Some of them experienced the Great Depression and World War II and were, for the most part, raised with the traditional home and family values. They experienced fewer opportunities in education, as well as in male-dominated professions such as medicine, law, and business (Kessler-Harris, 1982). These older women came of age during a period in which patriotism and national consensus flourished. Traditional values have been explicated as revolving around the family, love of country, competition, conformity, and authority (Gribbon, 1981). It should be noted that when earlier studies on midlife were conducted in the 1950s and 1960s, women did not generally participate in roles outside the home. However, the seeds of unrest were festering, and many women were experiencing dissatisfaction at not being self-actualized because they were unable to participate in the outside world (Friedan, 1963). Ehrenreich (1983), you will recall, relates that men in those years were expected to be the sole breadwinners in the family while their wives were expected to follow the traditional patterns of early marriage, childbearing, and child-rearing.

Theoretical Discussion

Midlife is the term used to describe a period in the adult life cycle when certain developmental landmarks occur. Among these are reflection upon one's mortality and life's limits, thought to occur sometime during the mid-30s (Sheehy, 1976). The actual age varies according to cultural and other factors, which designate midlife dependent on the theories set forth by disparate researchers. Erikson (1950) defines the middle years in terms of eight phases in the life cycle in which specific requisites are necessary in order to progress through the transition in an adaptive manner. Gould (1978) speaks of an inner-directedness, a focus on self, which designates midlife and assigns these events to the fortieth decade. Jung (1961), whose influence is found in Gould's work, suggests that a feeling of inner uncertainty prevails during an individual's mid to late 30s. Because of the power and numbers of the baby boomers, previous theories about the midlife transition will no doubt be impacted by what has happened to this cohort.

Problem

The dramatic increase in the number of contemporary women between the ages of 35 and 47 has far-reaching implications. This largest cohort in the population is rapidly advancing into middle age. Silverstone and Hyman (1982) refer to the midlife generation as the *sandwich generation,* those in between the younger generation on one side and the elder generation on the other. Furthermore, Silverstone concurs that there is a lack of knowledge because empirical studies on midlife are negligible. Davis (1981) reported that it has only been recently that the middle years have been recognized as pivotal, encompassing numerous life transitions, and *not* uneventful as previously believed. Models and norms of behavior for this life transition are slowly emerging. However, the newest cohort of midlife women may be quite divergent in light of how they were socialized and how they accepted new roles and adjustments to societal norms. The most recent participants in the midlife transition may find themselves ambivalent, allowing for the possibility of being in high states of anxiety because of their nontraditional lifestyles, which include postponement of marriage and childbearing and working in previously male-dominated spheres. As a result of the ambivalence and anxiety that may be present, it is significant to compare the baby-boom group of midlife women to an older sample of midlife women.

In my study, the scores of all of the participants who completed the State-Trait Anxiety Inventory (Spielberger, Gorsuch, & Luchene, 1983) and the Salamon-Conte Life Satisfaction Scale (1984) were analyzed and the age groups compared in order to help explain how socialization and social change may have influenced anxiety and life satisfaction in each of the groups. In addition, a demographic survey generated by the existing literature elicited lifestyle information about each of the participants in the study. Separating the effects that aging and maturity have on how persons perceive their own levels of satisfaction was an important task in the study. In the study, comparisons were made between the older and younger participants in order to describe how the various year groups are similar and different from one another. The comparisons were made by separating and analyzing the baby-boom and the pre-baby-boom cohorts.

Major Questions

1. Do baby-boom, college-educated, midlife women experience lower levels of life satisfaction and anxiety than pre-baby-boom women, as measured by the Salamon-Conte Life Satisfaction Scale and the State-Trait Anxiety Inventory (STAI) (Spielberger et al., 1983)?
2. What are the determinants of life satisfaction and anxiety in the baby-boom and pre-baby-boom midlife women?

Other Research Questions

3. What is the level of life satisfaction with regard to the stated lifestyle variables such as marital status, work role, and family income reported by the cohorts of the baby-boom and pre-baby-boom midlife women?
4. What is the relationship between life satisfaction and anxiety between each of the year groups?
5. What is the relationship between present socioeconomic status (SES) and life satisfaction?
6. What is the level of family solidarity (or divorce) with regard to self-reported life satisfaction?
7. What is the level of parental responsibility indicated by the various groups of midlife women?
8. What proportion of the baby-boom women work for wages outside the home?

9. Do the women in the sample experience a higher level of work satisfaction if they work for wages outside the home?

Hypotheses

Note: All measures have been calculated at the .05 level of significance when applicable.

1. High anxiety in midlife women who are ages 35 to 55 is related to a low level of life satisfaction.
2. The baby-boom women have significantly higher levels of anxiety than the pre-baby-boom cohort.
3. The baby-boom cohort will experience a lower level of life satisfaction than the older group of midlife women.
4. The following demographic variables are positively associated with life satisfaction: job status, the presence of children, marriage, extended family, general health status, culture/ethnicity, political activism, and family background.
5. The following demographic variables are negatively associated with life satisfaction: divorce, never having been married, the absence of children, and responsibility for elderly parents.

It will become evident as you read further that hypotheses two and three were disproved. The age factor was not relevent in this sample of baby-boom and pre-baby-boom women. Both age groups had high measures of life satisfaction and low measures of anxiety.

Importance of the Study

The study is important for two reasons. First, it presents information about the baby-boom generation who have recently entered the midlife transition. This newest cohort of midlife women was socialized during a period of great national upheaval in which the sexual revolution, the women's movement, and numerous other societal changes occurred. Changes related to these events are not well understood, nor has their impact on the pivotal midlife transition been studied. The literature reflects inconsistency in its treatment of the baby-boom midlife women. Some researchers have suggested that the younger cohort of midlife women has achieved a high level of life satisfaction because of the numerous opportunities that they have been given (Friedan, 1981; Wheeler, Lee, & Hardy, 1983). Others report that this cohort is highly stressed because of the multiple roles that they must play (Naisbitt, 1982; Jones, 1981). Secondly, older midlife women have been negatively portrayed as being highly anxious in previous, and possibly biased, research. Investigating evolving behavioral norms will enable us to determine whether the trend toward refuting the earlier studies portraying midlife women in a negative light will hold for the baby boomers. They have reportedly experienced self-fulfillment and have higher levels of life satisfaction. Nevertheless, additional stress and anxiety in their lives due to the multiple societal roles that they have adopted may be present. It is expected that new criteria will emerge from this and other studies that show lowered levels of anxiety in midlife women as a result of adaptation to life stressors as indicated by Selye (1955).

Definition of Terms

Midlife Transition   The portion of the life cycle between ages 35 and 65 as defined by a consensus of adult developmental researchers (Sheehy, 1976). Neugarten (1968) presents the following parameters:

1. Launching the children from the home (this may be different for the baby-boom generation who married later and postponed childbearing).
2. Reaching a peak in one's occupation.
3. Menopause (usually around age 45 or 50).
4. Grandparenthood.
5. Retirement.
6. Chronic illness onset.
7. Widowhood.

It will be interesting to determine if these markers are even relevant for the baby-boom generation.

Anxiety   A state that occurs when there is a lowering of the adaptive responses. When high levels of anxiety are experienced, problem solving and other activities tend to become rigid and inflexible (Adams, Hayes, & Hopson, 1977). Anxiety is also conceptualized as a transitory state in which feelings of tension and apprehension are present (Spielberger et al., 1983). The STAI provides data regarding this variable.

Life Satisfaction   A feeling of well-being and perceived success in one's undertakings. When this occurs, a feeling of self-fulfillment is present. This is usually associated with a strong sense of self-worth and autonomy (Krueger, 1984). Data regarding this variable was obtained from the Life Satisfaction Scale (Salamon & Conte, 1984).

Baby-Boom Generation   The generation born after World War II. It began in 1946, peaked in 1957, and ended in 1964. Some 76,441,000 babies were born during these 19 years (Jones, 1981). The oldest female members are now in their mid-30s and late 40s. During the time of the study, the oldest baby-boom midlife women were 42 to 43 years old. I have conducted two unpublished, subsequent studies on lifestyle and health practices of midlife baby-boom women and their older cohorts. Similar findings appear to replicate many of those from the earlier study that will be reported here.

The Variables

The major research questions sought to answer whether age was a factor in determining life satisfaction and anxiety. Subsequent to this, a series of other research questions were generated by the literature and operationalized by a demographic survey.

The demographic, life satisfaction, and anxiety variables were crosstabulated for each of the groups and the results were compared. Each of the research questions was converted into a measurable variable in statistical analysis.

Raw scores for levels of anxiety, measured by the State-Trait Anxiety Inventory (Spielberger et al., 1983), were ultimately scaled high, medium, and low. Raw scores for life satisfaction were measured by the Life Satisfaction Scale (Salamon-Conte, 1984) and were also scaled high, medium, and low.

The demographic questionnaire was based on the questions generated by the theories set forth in the literature on midlife women. These data were compressed, quantified, and coded to facilitate easier management of the analysis.

An explanation about the rationale for the selection of each of the variables follows.

Race   Rationale: To explore how minority and ethnic individuals might differ from the majority and to formulate a cultural perspective on each of the individuals. Life satisfaction and anxiety were also expected to be affected by this variable. A question of income level is also related to ethnicity. Horowitz-Lefkowitz (1984) speaks to increase educational opportunities for women, including minority women. Jones (1981) added that there was a greater tolerance for minorities noted among the baby-boom generation. These factors would suggest an increase in the numbers of minorities among the baby-boom women in this study. Stress among minority groups is another component of this question and was addressed in *Enduring Legacies* (1987).

Religious Preference   Rationale: To understand whether religious beliefs and practice equated with life satisfaction and low levels of anxiety.
In addition, religious trends were explored. The question of how religion
affects the cohorts in question is addressed in *Enduring Legacies* (1987) and
is reflective of a return to God and organized religion. The baby-boom generation is seen as becoming increasingly conservative in all aspects of life
as they become reflective and search for life's meaning. In addition, White
(1986) reports on a national trend of charitable behavior substantiated by
an increase in volunteerism and charitable contributions.

Urban, Suburban, or Rural   Rationale: A purely demographic question
to determine the diversity of the sample.

Marital Status   Rationale: Measures of marital status were expected
to relate to anxiety and life satisfaction, and were also instrumental in identifying trends and societal changes. Krantzler (1981) and others suggest a
return to the traditional values of marriage and family, and it was projected that this sample would espouse those values as well. New norms
are emerging as many women are opting for a combination of homemaking and employment outside the home. Dual family income has become
an economic necessity for many families. The question of whether this will
lead to a more stressful lifestyle or whether it will equate with increased
life satisfaction is relevant for the cohort of midlife women in this study.

Level of Education   Rationale: Based on the literature, it was expected
that the trend for the baby-boom women to have increased educational opportunities would hold. This also permitted comparison to the pre-baby-
boom sample. The price of expanded opportunities in education and the
resulting high-power career choices may prove to be a liability for some
baby-boom midlife women. Many of these women find themselves facing
the limits of the biological clock without the self-fulfillment of marriage and
children. Friedan (1981) has noted this apparent subtle change in values
among baby-boom women. For many in the older cohort, a more traditional
lifestyle was the only option as they were socialized (Rubin, 1979).

Spouse/Partner Employment Status   Rationale: This was important in discovering trends relating to work history and role sharing and comparing the
experiences of each of the age groups. All of these factors were expected to
relate to life satisfaction and anxiety in a positive manner except when there
was a role overload or dissatisfaction in the workplace. Other factors, such
as the societal trend toward a huge increase in the numbers of women in the
work force, are also addressed by Schwartz (1989). Most of the college-
educated women noted in her research have chosen to have it all, suggestive

of marriage and children in conjunction with a successful career. Admonition is made to industry to be cognizant of this valuable resource and to provide support for working women. On the home front, two-income families are the norm, but most studies show that the male spouse does not participate equally in household chores. It remains to be seen whether perceived stress and anxiety results in lower life satisfaction as a result.

Children   Rationale: Based on the literature, child-rearing was expected to be different for each of the groups. It was explored to examine emerging trends and its effect on measures of life satisfaction and anxiety. As a result of the birth control pill, the option to choose to bear children is a relatively new phenomenon to be addressed by baby-boom women. Large numbers of baby-boom women are choosing to bear children, although the trend appears to be for smaller families and childbearing later in life than their predecessors (The New Baby Bloom, 1982). McKinlay and McKinlay (1986) reported that, in their study, older midlife women reported high stress when adult children returned home following divorce or for economic reasons. This is probably not an issue for midlife women with younger families. However, because of the increase in blended families following divorce, even younger women may face this dilemma as step-parents.

Assistance with Child Care   Rationale: Previously, it was customary for the extended family to assist in child-rearing, but currently the literature disputes this as the society becomes increasingly mobile. New trends are also emerging in relation to marital status, late childbearing, and unavailable grandmothers who may be in the work force as well.

Present Socioeconomic Status

Employment   Rationale: This may be an instance where age becomes the discriminating factor. The oldest women in the study may have retired from the work force or may have decided not to work because their household income was sufficient. Many of the women in this older group may harbor a more traditional perspective of homemaking and volunteerism rather than employment outside the home. The younger women in the study are expected to be involved in less traditional professions because they encountered greater educational and career opportunities than their predecessors.

Household Income   Rationale: The literature suggests that the baby-boom generation was raised in more affluent surroundings than their predecessors and many societal structures were changed in the process. It was of interest to inquire whether the baby-boom women in this sample were better off financially than their predecessors, and whether or not this equated with life satisfaction and level of anxiety.

Financial Status Compared to Parents   Rationale: It was also of interest to understand whether baby-boom women perceive that they were better off than their parents. The older cohort was expected to be ahead of the baby-boom women and their own parents in financial gain. It is theorized that this is so because the older cohort has enjoyed prosperity during an extended affluence period, and because they, or their spouses, are currently in their prime earning years.

Miscellaneous Variables

Volunteer Activities   Rationale: So much has been attributed to the me generation, the baby boomers, that it was of interest to know whether this group was indeed hedonistic and uncaring, how they compared to their predecessors, and whether helping others made them happy and satisfied.

Political Preference   Rationale: Two questions in the demographic survey were based on the General Social Survey (1972–1987) for the purpose of comparing national data to this sample of midlife women. Active participation in the political system is seen as a relevant variable because some individuals in the baby-boom generation, as they reached their twenties, dropped out of mainstream society in protest of existing social values (Lewin & Spates, 1970).

Elderly Parents' Demands   Rationale: The literature suggests that midlife children are usually expected to assist their elderly parents as they become infirm (Silverstone & Hyman, 1982). However, for many of the older members in the sample whose parents may be deceased, this may not be an issue. The younger cohort of baby-boom women, on the other hand, may have healthy, fairly young parents, who are in good health and have not yet become infirm.

Physical Health and Regular Exercise   Rationale: General health status is equated with life satisfaction, was measured with the life satisfaction scale, and was implied in the exercise question on the demographic survey. This facilitated measurement of current trends toward increased health promotion. Jones (1981) speaks of a cohort of baby boomers who sought self-help and healing following the early years of upheaval and turmoil. An expansion of participation in physical exercise was a direct result of this. The high cost of medical care and the new emphasis on re-sponsibility for one's own well-being is influencing this variable in all age groups (Birren, Kinney, Shaie, & Woodruff, 1981).

Procedures for Data Collection

Prior to the implementation of the study, a proposal was submitted to the university of choice for approval. The Office of Alumni Affairs supported the project and agreed to generate a random sample of 130 individuals in each of the 21 requested graduating year groups between 1955 and 1975. In addition, they agreed to supply mailing labels for each of the randomly selected female graduates.

The process of assembling the materials for the mailing packet for each of the selected alumna was a gigantic task. In all, 2,730 packets were as-sembled. Included in each packet was a cover letter, a demographic sur-vey, an anxiety inventory, a life satisfaction scale, and a self-addressed, stamped envelope.

Treatment of the Data and Response Rate

The data source was the response from the mailed questionnaires. The mailing to the 2,730 randomly selected midlife women from the 21 gradu-ating classes of the university yielded 1,070 responses from California and virtually every other state in the United States. The response from each of three artificially divided age groups was relatively constant. The des-ignations were:

Age Group 1 (ages 35 to 42 consisted of 326 baby-boom women).
Age Group 2 (ages 43 to 48 encompassed 292 pre-baby-boom mid-midlife women).
Age Group 3 (ages 49 to 55 presented with 344 older pre-baby-boom midlife women).

In addition, three 10-year age groups (ages 35, 45, and 55) were analyzed for validation of the findings.

There were 159 returns from out of state and the remainder were from California. Thirty-six surveys were returned by the postal service with no forwarding address. Overall, this constituted a return rate of 41%. Another 108 of the returned surveys were ineligible because the respondents were not within the parameters set for the study. In all, there were 962 eligible subjects whose responses were included in the final analysis.

All of the nominal variables in the demographic survey were converted to numerical values and coded appropriately. In the case of ordinal data, the rank orders were coded from high to low for ease of interpretation. When all of the data were collected, they were entered into the computer using the Crunch Statistical Package (1987). This computer program has been designed to free the researcher from the mechanics of the analysis, while encouraging examination of the data from different perspectives. Means, frequencies, standard deviations, and cross-tabulation are only a part of the program's capability. Analysis of the variance described the differences between the older and younger cohorts in the sample. The data served to explain phenomena, but no causal model was tested. The measures also served to identify subcases to investigate further, summarize, and draw conclusions about similarities and differences between the groups.

All of the variables were analyzed initially by computing means and obtaining a correlation coefficient to determine differences and similarities between the groups. Analysis of variance was conducted on relevant independent variables to determine with statistical significance their effect on the three major dependent variables of anxiety state, anxiety trait, and life satisfaction. In addition, a linear regression analysis was plotted on appropriate data. Some of the variables were cross-tabulated for frequencies and percentages and in some instances bar graphs were used to illustrate percentage variation.

The Instruments

The Anxiety Inventory

Before 1950, there was little empirical research on the subject of anxiety, resulting in a lack of effective instruments that could adequately measure anxiety levels. Spielberger, Gorsuch, and Luchene (1983) elaborated on the initial work on anxiety first presented by Cattell (1966), who first developed the State-Trait Anxiety Inventory in 1970. Since then, numerous refinements to the original instrument have been rendered based on research using normal adult and adolescent populations. Each revision has served to develop a more pure anxiety measure, which deleted any reference to depression. An effort was also made to have a more universally acceptable format that would relate to individuals with lower levels of education. The self-reporting scale has been utilized in over 2,000 studies, has been printed in 30 languages, and has become a well-respected measure of anxiety in many settings.

Normative data supplied with the instrument are reflective mainly of trait anxiety, which is highly correlated to anxiety state. Samples consisting of working adults, college students, high school students, and military recruits created the norms for trait anxiety. State anxiety norms were validated using samples of general medical and surgical patients, young prisoners, and neuropsychiatric patients. The authors acknowledge that, while the sampling is not representative, it is comparable to scores reported by other researchers who used the STAI. One such study was conducted on 1,838 employees of the Federal Aviation Administration (Spielberger et al., 1983).

The inventory is based on the premise that an emotional state exists at a given moment in time and at a particular level of interest. Anxiety states are characterized by "subjective feelings of tension, apprehension, nervousness, worry, and by activation or arousal of the autonomic nervous system" (Spielberger et al., 1983, p. 1). There are two parts to the instrument. The state anxiety reflects transitory feelings of worry and apprehension. The trait anxiety portion reflects the personality trait itself, which is enduring in dealing with all anxiety-provoking situations. The anxiety trait score is predictive of how an individual will experience state anxiety during a threatening situation. In addition, the trait measurement has also been effective in measuring depression, which has sometimes been attributed to women in the midlife transition.

Clear instructions were printed on both sides of the one page test, and individuals were asked to describe the frequency and intensity of how they generally feel and how they feel at a particular moment in time. The test took roughly 15 minutes to complete and the respondents were asked such questions as "I feel upset" or "I feel calm" to test how one feels at that moment in time. This revealed a score for anxiety state. Examples of questions relating to anxiety trait were "I am usually calm" or "I am usually happy."

Life Satisfaction Scale

A measure of life satisfaction, a representative measure of well-being, is found in the Salamon-Conte Life Satisfaction in the Elderly Scale (LSS) (1984). The LSS was developed based on the existing literature in the field, most notably the work of Neugarten, Havighurst, and Tobin (1961). Their work is reflective of successful aging with clearly defined life satisfaction constructs such as pleasure in daily activities, a meaningful life, achievement of goals, a positive outlook on life, and a high level of self-concept. However, this earlier work presented with very little reliability and validation data. Salamon-Conte (1984) posited that more than the original five constructs were necessary to adequately assess life satisfaction. To that end, they developed the LSS, which incorporated all of the previously suggested constructs (Neugarten et al., 1961) and added the three additional constructs of health, finances, and social contacts. The self-evaluating pencil test consists of 40 questions in which five questions were generated for each of the eight constructs. A high score indicates high life satisfaction, while a low score reflects the reverse.

Reliability measurements of the scale were conducted initially on numerous individuals ages 55 to 90. Validation of the Life Satisfaction Scale used several multivariate approaches such as Cattell's SCREE Test (1978) and factor analysis with high correlation noted in all categories (Salamon-Conte, 1984).

The normative data presented by Salamon-Conte are preliminary because of the relatively small sample used during the early development of the instrument. This is attributed to the recency of the development of the instrument at the time that this study was conducted. However, the tool was developed with a strong theoretical and parsimonious base relating to the measure of life satisfaction. Scores noted in this study are consistent with the norms suggested by the instrument, and high levels of life satisfaction appear to correlate with low anxiety levels. Examples of the questions on the life satisfaction scale are "Physically, I am: unhealthy, somewhat unhealthy, average, healthy, very healthy." Another question is "My schedule of activities is: very unsatisfying, not really satisfying, occasionally satisfying, satisfying, very satisfying."

Delimitations of the Study

The data generated in the study describe those midlife women in the cohort of interest who were graduates of the same university. Additional empirical studies should be undertaken in order to create generalizations and representative data about the larger universe of midlife women.

The parameters of the study were the female graduates of a southern California university who were born between 1933 and 1953. The sample encompassed both midlife women from the baby-boom generation as well as those who preceded them. Because the study is concerned with information about college-educated women, information about non-college-educated women is lacking.

Limitations of the Study

Because of the passage of time and loss of contact with the alumni, current names and addresses of 33 of the alumna were unavailable and their packets were returned. Several surveys were deemed ineligible. In one instance, a male alumni was randomly selected because of his dual-gender name. The alumni wife offered to respond to the survey, but she was not eligible because she had graduated from another university. Two of those selected to participate were deceased, and their surveys were returned by family members.

Assumptions of the Study

Individuals who receive the surveys may choose not to answer the request. This may result in bias and make the results ungeneralizable. However, there is some dispute as to what constitutes an adequate rate of return. Mailed surveys rarely achieve more than a 50% return (Miller, 1982). A 41% return was realized in this study.

High life satisfaction and low anxiety levels indicate adaptive coping mechanisms, while low life satisfaction and high anxiety levels may reflect the opposite. Ultimately, these findings will have implications for adaptation in later life as well.

Results

The knowledge gleaned in this study about college-educated midlife women with regard to lifestyle, marital status, work roles, and the like has yielded some surprises. While a variety of the results do support and confirm certain established trends, other results reveal unexpected directions in the behavior of midlife women, which may be a direct consequence of changes in societal norms over the past several decades.

An unexpected dividend from the returns was the outpouring of personal comments and feelings expressed by the women who answered the survey. Their responses were rich and diverse. Some of the notes and letters were heartwarming, displaying enormous courage and strength, while others were humorous. Many are relevant to the independent variables and are integrated throughout the chapter.

Investigating the Age Factor

Initially, it was hypothesized that age would be the major factor in determining high life satisfaction and low anxiety. This, I hypothesized, was because the baby-boom women, juggling work and family obligations, would have higher anxiety levels and lower life satisfaction than their older counterparts. In addition, I hypothesized that the pre-baby-boom groups of women would have lower anxiety than the baby-boom cohort because of the older women's presumably better-developed coping skills. Well, I was wrong.

Certainly, one of the most surprising results of the study was that neither age nor historical events such as the Great Depression, the civil rights movement, or the sexual revolution appeared to be significant in causing differences in life satisfaction, anxiety state, or anxiety trait. When age was the independent variable and anxiety state (ANXS), anxiety trait (ANXT), and life satisfaction (LS) were the dependent variables, there were no significant differences among the three age groups. This finding was replicated when the 35-, 45-, and 55-year-olds' scores were isolated and analyzed. The three testing variables showed no significant variation when analysis of variance were conducted. High scores reflecting high anxiety on both of the anxiety measures were set at 34, and low scores (below 150) on life satisfaction reflect a low life satisfaction. While not significant, older midlife women showed slightly higher anxiety levels and lower life satisfaction levels.

Even the linear regression relationships between ANXS, ANXT, and LS are essentially the same with respect to the age groups. This says that the relationship, for instance, between life satisfaction and anxiety trait that each age group experiences is nearly identical. In other words, as anxiety declines, life satisfaction increases.

These women eloquently elaborated on being satisfied with their life situations. One woman said, "I am very attractive, but not compared to a 20-year-old." From a 40-year-old, "Some of us have managed a home, family, and career before the modern woman came along." This 54-year-old, however, says it all, "I happen to be in love and everything seems possible."

Anxiety and stress in everyday life was expressed by a woman who claimed that she was anxious because "I had a bad week, I just paid my income tax, had the car break down, and I had to put the cat to sleep."

It was originally anticipated that it would be difficult to separate the effects of age from historical events. With the unexpected result of similarity among the age groups, it became evident that the other factors mentioned previously in this chapter had to be explored in order to find significant variation in ANXS, ANXT, and LS. If these women were all relatively free from anxiety and had a high level of life satisfaction, I needed to discover what other factors made them happy or sad and what made them anxious and stressed.

Identifying the Significant Variables

The first major task was to determine the specific demographic variables responsible for significant variation in anxiety state *or* how one feels at this particular moment in time, anxiety trait *or* how one usually feels (Spielberger et al., 1983), and life satisfaction (Salamon-Conte, 1984).

Cross-Tabulation Results

Cross-tabulation permitted a vehicle for examination of the individual age groups designated as AGE1 (ages 35 to 42, the baby boomers), AGE2 (ages 43 to 48, mid pre-baby boomers), and AGE3 (ages 49 to 55, the oldest of the pre-baby boomers). It was determined that age groups exhibited similar behavior with respect to a significant variable if the distribution within each age group was the same across the age groups. Otherwise, it was concluded that there were notable differences between the age groups.

It was essential to question how each significant variable distributes itself among the different age groups. In the final analysis, all the differences and similarities must even out and compensate for each other. Otherwise, the different age groups would feel differently about life satisfaction, anxiety state, and anxiety trait. A discussion of similarities and differences between the age groups is shown here.

Similarities

1. *Current Marital Status*

	(Ages 35–42)	(Ages 43–48)	(Ages 49–55)
Married	67.47%	71.62%	72.83%

The majority of the participants were married.

2. *Household Income*   among the three groups was relatively the same. This was rather unexpected since the younger groups are usually attributed to being behind their older counterparts in household income. The numbers are presented in percentages and actual number of individuals in each income group.

   * n = the number of subjects in each age group*
   * Please note that the columns will be in the same order throughout these discussions.

	Age Group 1 n=326	Age Group 2 n=292	Age Group 3 n=344
<$25000	5.21% (17)	3.08% (9)	5.23% (18)
$25000–$49999	25.77% (84)	18.49% (54)	22.38% (77)

	Age Group 1 n=326	Age Group 2 n=292	Age Group 3 n=344
$50000–$74999	23.31% (76)	22.26% (65)	23.26% (80)
$75000–$99999	14.11% (46)	18.15% (53)	14.83% (51)
$100000–$149999	18.40% (60)	19.18% (56)	19.48% (67)
>$150000	13.19% (43)	18.84% (55)	14.83% (51)

3. *Enjoyment of Employment*

Yes	84.59%	81.14%	76.55%

It is interesting to note that the baby-boom women were the most satisfied group.

4. *Reasons Not Currently Employed*

Homemaking	14.46%	13.20%	14.44%

This was the factor most noted as a reason for not being employed at the present.

5. *Parental Influence*   (encouragement to work following college graduation)

Yes	85.93%	81.54%	79.83%

This may reflect a parental expectation that one should be encouraged to work following a four-year college education. There is a trend toward more encouragement as the cohorts become younger. You will recall that older midlife women where not expected by their parents to join the work force.

6. *Reentry into the Work Force with Children*   (before children went to school)

21.58%	21.78%	21.97%

This was a surprising and very traditional value that was consistent across all of the age groups indicating that only around 21% of the women chose to return to work prior to their children entering school.

7. *Participation in Volunteer Activities*

59.63%	63.37%	60.17%

This finding appears to contradict the popularly held belief that the baby boomers are a self-centered cohort. In this study at least, the majority participate in some form of volunteer activity. In fact, in all of the three groups in this study, the rates are certainly comparable to each other.

8. *Regular Exercise*

Yes	60.37%	66.89%	65.34%

This finding was a surprise. Although all three of the groups display high levels of participation in regular exercise, the baby-boom women exercised the least.

Differences

1. *Race* Diversity has changed with each progressive age group as minority groups have increasingly been given the opportunity to attend institutions of higher education. It is interesting to see the diversity begin to increase progressively with each subsequent age cohort. However, Caucasians continue to dominate the higher-education scene. The positive trend is that minority participation slowly continues to increase in the 1990s. Hispanic women in the study reported the lowest scores on life satisfaction. Since there were only 16 individuals in this category, statistical significance cannot be claimed.

Asian	8.73% (29)	5.30% (16)	3.37% (12)
Black	3.31% (11)	2.32% (7)	0.84% (3)
Caucasian	84.94% (282)	90.73% (274)	94.38% (336)
Hispanic	2.71% (9)	0.66% (2)	1.40% (5)

One of the respondents when asked about her race replied that she was a member of the *human* race. Insight such as this, exercised by all members of society, might inspire us to be free from prejudice and discrimination.

2. *Current Marital Status*

Never Married	20%	7%	3%
Widowed	0%	3%	3%
Divorced	8%	14%	17%
Separated	2%	1%	2%
Living Together	2%	3%	3%
Married	68%	72%	72%

Clearly, baby-boom women are the least married and the most single of all of the groups. This is reflective of the trend toward later marriage or choosing to remain single. It is interesting to note that those women who reported that they were married or in committed relationships were the happiest and the least anxious. In opposition to these feelings were divorced or never married women. Curiously, the widowed women in the study claim relatively high life satisfaction and low anxiety. This is especially true for widows who have adapted and made a life for themselves in the work force and/or with family and friends.

3. *Living Together before Marriage*   This was another surprise because of the increased sexual freedom attributed to the baby-boom generation. Although percentages of baby boomers choosing to live together before marriage are relatively higher than for the other groups, it was interesting to note that for the majority of the baby-boom women this lifestyle choice was not generally chosen. However, two women who chose this alternative made the following remarks. One 44-year-old, married three times, had lived with two different men before marriage and said that she wouldn't do it again. Another wrote that she lived with someone before marriage, but not with her present husband.

4. *Number of Times Divorced and Remarried*

Not Applicable	82.48%	70.96%	69.30%
Once	8.76%	13.20%	12.96%
Twice	0.60%	3.30%	2.82%

* additional remarriages were not of sufficient number to mention

It should be noted here that baby-boom women have tended to marry later and may not have divorced as frequently as their older counterparts at the point in time when they completed the survey.

5. *Number of Children*

None	43.23%	21.78%	12.04%
One	15.69%	15.18%	8.96%
Two	33.85%	38.94%	42.58%
Three	7.38%	17.16%	23.81%
Four	1.23%	4.95%	8.12%

*additional children were not of sufficient number to mention

The trends in this study mirror those for society in general with regard to family size in each of the age groups. You will note a gradual decline in family size and that the baby-boom women displayed greatest proportion of never having children.

6. *Family Assistance with Children*   (grandparents and other extended family)

Yes	32.12%	37.62%	43.73%

This is reflective, as mentioned previously, of the trend toward later marriage, a more mobile society, and the changing roles of women and grandmothers.

7. *Employment while Child-Rearing*

Yes	46.67%	55.78%	56.06%

One 42-year-old woman wrote that she had recently returned to work following the birth of her child who was now 18 months. She may be a model for how postponement of childbearing affects career-minded contemporary women. At least two women in their 40s, who had never married and were enjoying successful careers, reported that they were single parents with one child each. Social acceptance toward single parenthood in unmarried career women is a trend in evidence here. It is also interesting to note that over half of the older midlife women were employed during child-rearing. The baby-boom cohort had a lower overall percentage, probably because so many of them have never had children.

8. *Reentry into the Work Force while Child-Rearing* (when the children were in school)

6.69%	29.37%	32.11%

The baby-boom group had fewer children so this may not have been an issue. It is obvious that less than one third of the older women in the study chose this option.

9. *Other Reasons Not Currently Employed*

Health	0.30%	0.66%	1.12%
Prefer Not To	0.30%	1.65%	5.62%

These findings may reflect the age factor. More older women preferred not to work than the younger cohort.

10. *Empty Nest Following Child-Rearing* This became most relevant for the older pre-baby-boom cohort.

Yes	0.30%	12.25%	46.48%

In dealing with empty nest issues and her husband's midlife career change, this was reported. "My husband is taking a leave of absence from his law practice, forcing me to terminate an eight-year real estate career because of a move to a new location." Missing her daughter, who had left for college, was an additional loss felt by this woman. Perhaps if her life had remained stable when her child left the nest, this would not be an issue.

11. *Political Orientation* Although there are some similarities noted here, the differences are most pronounced with regard to a more liberal, middle-of-the-road orientation in the younger age group. The younger group also displayed a slightly lower percentage in the conservative category.

Extremely Liberal	2.43%	2.32%	1.14%
Liberal	17.63%	14.19%	10.80%
Slightly Liberal	13.68%	14.85%	9.94%
Middle-of-the-Road	16.72%	13.53%	14.20%
Slightly Conservative	22.80%	24.42%	23.58%
Conservative	23.40%	27.39%	32.10%
Extremely Conservative	1.52%	1.65%	5.40%
Not Sure	1.82%	1.65%	2.84%

It is clear that the baby-boom women were the most liberal of the groups, but it is of interest to note that liberalism appears to decline with age. It is somewhat puzzling that those who were undecided or liberal in their political orientation indicated that they were the least satisfied, and scored lower on measures of life satisfaction. Levity was obvious when a 41-year-old was asked about her political preferences and she related that "I do not vote for women, blacks, men, or turnips, I vote for individuals."

12. *Change in Political Views with Age* illustrates that the younger group became less liberal with age than the other two age groups. This is also reflective of a movement toward a trend away from the liberal perspective as one ages. Surprisingly, change in political orientation toward becoming more conservative was also calculated, with significance, with lower life satisfaction scores.

More Liberal	20.30%	33.67%	31.81%
Less Liberal	40.61%	36.00%	32.09%
No Change	39.09%	30.33%	36.10%

Significant Independent Variables

Upon investigation of the statistical findings, the following independent variables were isolated as having had a significant effect on the two measures of anxiety and life satisfaction. Significance in the Analysis of Variance (ANOVA) on all of the variance measures was set at the .05 level of probability.

Household Income (HI) was found to have the greatest influence on life satisfaction (LS) and anxiety (ANXS and ANXT) of all of the variables. Moreover, across all of the age groups, the following findings were nearly identical. High level of income yielded high scores on life satisfaction and low scores on anxiety, while low income levels revealed the opposite. The greater the income, the greater the sense of well-being on all measures. In this sample of midlife women, having a high income (above $75,000) made people happy and less anxious. The women in the study have remained consistent with their older cohorts in household income. All of the groups had similar income levels. The difference is that many of the baby-boom women have participated in the work force and have achieved high-level dual-income households.

Several comments presented here represent a new perspective on the implications and expectations of household income. A 36-year-old who makes less money than her husband is feeling uneasy because she feels "sexism is keeping us from the top." She goes on to observe that many women are being driven out of the work force as a result of corporate mergers and the like. Dealing with the problem of being the sole family supporter while her husband begins a new business is difficult for her. She is trying to understand how money should be managed in her family. She expressed the fact that "money is power": the more money you have, the more power you have.

Financial security was on the mind of another woman who remarked about her recent divorce that, after a 17-year marriage and a custody battle, she had entered *instant poverty*. She had gone from upwards of $250,000 a year to $40,000, certainly not *poverty*, but still a tragic blow to her former lifestyle.

Finally, this dramatic lifestyle change from a woman who told about a midlife career change. Both she and her husband are quitting their professions after 25 years. They purchased a million dollar mobile home park that they will manage. They are hoping to make ends meet so that they can pay college tuition for their two sons.

Participating in Regular Exercise   was yet another independent variable that produced significant variation among LS, ANXS, and ANXT. In addition, those who exercised regularly were significantly happier than those who did not. It was found that if one participates in regular exercise it can lead one to a happier, healthier life.

The next five independent variables that affected LS, ANXT, and ANXS when analysis of variance was applied all relate to survey questions regarding marriage and child-rearing. Those women in the survey who did not espouse a traditional lifestyle incorporating marriage and child-rearing, or those women who were divorced, were most adversely impacted with regard to being satisfied with their lives. This analysis of *never having been married* revealed both low life satisfaction and high anxiety levels. Life satisfaction scores for never married and divorced women were lower than for the other groups. Anxiety scores for never married women and divorced women were higher than in the other groups.

On her marriage, one woman wrote, "I wonder how many women are satisfied with their mates? My previous relationships were better, but I can't leave because of money, my age, and single life is lonely." Another explained that she had divorced and remarried the same man, she was busy and overextended, but that she was never bored. However, differences in life satisfaction between those who received parental encouragement and those who did not was not significant. This result suggests that one tends to perceive that a lack of parental encouragement contributes to a sense of anxiety but does not necessarily diminish overall life satisfaction. Remarking about parental influence, one woman stated, "I wanted to work; my parents never had to encourage me."

With respect to the other variables in this study, several interesting predicted trends were noted. First, those women who did not have children scored higher in anxiety and lower in life satisfaction. Perhaps societal demands toward the traditional expectation toward marriage and family are causing higher anxiety levels and low levels of life satisfaction. For example, a 45-year-old woman, who was making in excess of $100,000 a year, was about to be married for the first time. She related that she hoped that she would be able to have children. Seemingly, the biological clock has no limit for this woman.

When the issue of satisfaction with one's work was analyzed, it was interesting to note that those women who enjoyed their work scored highest in life satisfaction and had lower anxiety levels. Conversely, those women who answered that they were satisfied only sometimes or not at all registered higher in anxiety and lower in life satisfaction.

When reasons for not being currently employed were explored, those women who were not employed because of pressure from family or for health reasons were the least happy. Those who chose not to work, but opted for homemaking or retirement, appeared happy with their decisions as expressed by the pre-baby-boom women whose daughter *does it all* and says that her daughter is critical of her for not accomplishing more in her life. The mother says, "I never found homemaking boring." It should be noted that of the 962 women who answered this question, 768 were currently employed either part- or full-time, and all but 42 had been employed for various periods of time following college graduation.

Some pertinent comments follow. "I was content being a homemaker, but now everyone is harping on how unfulfilled I am. My husband says that he is tired of supporting me and wants me to earn my keep. I must now seek employment and the prospect is very depressing. My husband thinks we need a second income; he has so many plans and I am failing him." One can only question whether this is a prevailing attitude or something particular to this relationship.

One 40-year-old who hates to admit that she is just a homemaker said that she retired at 40 so that she could spend time with her children ages 9 and 11. Another former career woman added, "I have an MBA, but I am now a homemaker and mother of three children." For these and several other women in the study, it appears that family came before career, while others managed both work and children simultaneously.

Several other variables tested yielded small significance on the measures of anxiety and life satisfaction. Race was an issue that appeared to effect anxiety level, but not life satisfaction, except in the case of the small sample of Hispanic women.

Participation in volunteer activity was shown to be indicative of happier feelings with regard to low trait anxiety means and high life satisfaction means. As if to underscore the feelings expressed by many in the older cohort, a 54-year-old expressed, "I feel privileged to have grown up in changing times. None of us has it all. I would like to be more financially independent, but all in all I am satisfied. Satisfaction is now coming from love and giving service to others."

Those women whose parents required assistance showed a higher anxiety state significance than those who were not required to assist. Life satisfaction was not influenced by this variable. This may be explained by the fact that few in the study reported the necessity to care for relatively healthy and robust aging parents. It is conjectured that this finding will change as the cohorts age. However, due to increased longevity, the question of caring for aging parents may not be an issue for many years to come. One woman shared that all of the siblings in her family pooled their resources to purchase a home for their aging parents. This is in opposition to the feelings of another woman who believes that society does not adequately provide for the elderly.

The number of times a woman was divorced and remarried demonstrated only slight significance with regard to decreased life satisfaction. The least happy in the study were those who never remarried following divorce, and the four individuals who divorced and remarried three times. There were 730 women in the study who had never been divorced. Roughly 25% of the women in the study had been divorced at least once. This trend was lower than the national average reported to be 50%. Finally, the number of children was significant only in the measure of anxiety state. It appears that those with more than six children were most affected.

Analysis of Variance was also conducted on several other of the independent variables for the purpose of exploring whether there were any other variables that might influence anxiety or life satisfaction. There were no significant scores to illustrate variability of those with foreign-born parents, religious or nonreligious orientation, change from childhood religious orientation, participation in religious activity, or form of assistance required for parental needs. Some of the revelations about the religious practices of the group were rather surprising. Forty percent stated that they never went to church. This was higher than the reported 33% reported by the *Enduring Legacies* study (1987). Although there were at least 25 religions noted, this sample reflects a national trend toward more traditional values, including a return to religion. On religion, one woman noted that her childhood religion was "any local church," while another stated that she was a "laid-back Christian." Certainly, prior to the women's movement, a woman in the ministry was unheard of. Even more unique is the woman in this study who is not only in the ministry, but who also disclosed that she had been divorced twice.

In summary, it has been demonstrated that the variables contributing most significantly, positively or negatively, to one's level of either anxiety or life satisfaction are household income, regular exercise, marital status (being married related to low anxiety and high life satisfaction), bearing children, and enjoyment of one's occupation. Most importantly, these results hold true regardless of one's age.

Other Trends

This section describes trends that were evident when frequencies were run on some of the other demographic variables contained in the study.

1. Age of first marriage in the baby-boom group was higher than that in those older midlife women although the age at which the baby boomers peaked remained relatively similar.

Age Married	Baby Boomers	Pre-Baby Boomers
20	1.87%	3.48%
21	5.61%	8.94%
22	11.50%	17.27%
23 *peak age*	12.57%	18.03%
24	9.36%	11.82%
25	4.55%	7.73%
26	6.42%	4.24%
27	5.35%	2.58%
28	5.35%	3.33%
29	1.87%	2.42%
30	3.48%	1.36%
31	1.60%	1.06%
32	2.14%	1.52%

2. The popular notion that the baby boomers had more educational opportunities held true in this study. There were more doctorates and master's degrees noted in the baby-boom sample. To reflect this perspective on higher levels of education, the value placed on other women's achievement is evident here. This sense of increased opportunities for women was voiced by some of the women in the study who wrote to congratulate and encourage me in my own

research. One in particular admonished me to "Fight On," while another told me to "expect a miracle, work toward it, and it will be yours." A 39-year-old judge remarked, "It is a pleasure to see other women advancing and fulfilling their dreams." Several others were so enthusiastic about the project that they offered names and addresses of their friends who were alumna. Unfortunately, because of the randomness of the sample, it was not possible to include them in the survey.

3. When frequencies were run on types of occupations, great diversity was evident. Eighty-five different occupations were noted by the respondents. A listing of the most repeated occupations is presented here with percentages listed for each age group.

Occupation	Age Group 1	Age Group 2	Age Group 3
Teaching	24.70%	37.62%	34.45%
Occupational/			
Physical Therapy	8.13%	3.30%	4.48%
Law	6.63%	1.98%	0.84%
Administration	5.72%	1.98%	1.40%
Dental Hygiene	4.22%	6.27%	13.73%
Marketing	3.01%	3.30%	0.84%
President/Vice			
President Company	2.71%	1.65%	1.96%
School Administration	2.11%	4.62%	1.68%
Real Estate	1.81%	3.30%	3.92%
Office Manager	1.51%	2.97%	2.51%
Counseling	1.51%	2.97%	1.21%
Secretarial	0.90%	1.98%	1.96%
Nursing	0.60%	0.99%	1.96%
Professor	0.30%	2.97%	0.84%
Retail Manager	0.00%	0.33%	1.96%

In spite of the diversity of the many occupational categories, it should be noted that teaching remains the primary occupation for a large percentage of the women in the baby-boom age group. The percentage of women who choose to teach is slowly decreasing as women are moving gradually toward more nontraditional professional positions. To underscore the flight from the teaching profession, a 38-year-old woman recalled, "I feel that I am two people, one at home and one at work, with two full-time jobs. I enjoy working but I wish for more time for me; I am always doing for others. Marriage is okay but my teaching career is fraught with too many unpaid hours, too many students, no free time, too little respect, and 50 to 60 hours a week." Herein lies a clear indictment of the problems with the teaching profession, and a plausible reason that another woman gave for leaving teaching for a career in real estate. Another of the declining professions was commented on by one woman who stated that she left the dental hygiene profession because of the threat of AIDS.

I am including several quotes from some of the women who displayed an amazing amount of courage and fortitude as they make their way in the face of adversity. Their stories are an inspiration to all of us and reflect how they are striving to make a difference.

A moving note was written by a mother about her blind daughter, an alumna, who has reached great heights in her struggle for excellence. She wrote the answers to the survey for her daughter. She proudly related that her daughter, through scholarships, had attained a master's degree and achieved the highest grade point average of any student at her university. A plaque in her honor hangs at the university. The daughter at the time of the study was 40 years old, married, and the mother of two children. Her present position involves tutoring a blind student. She was formerly employed as a counselor for the probation department in her town.

Another woman wrote, "I continue to work as a computer and math teacher in addition to being the mother of two children, my youngest is two and a half, although I am a cancer patient. I was diagnosed 15 months ago and I had surgery and chemotherapy. I have a 50/50 chance of survival." So much is left unsaid by this 39-year-old woman, but the courage in these words is unmistakable.

A 49-year-old paraplegic writes, "I continue to work with the problems of life, living, and relationships." A 55-year-old explained, "I have lost my hearing and I am totally deaf, a recent turn. It has changed my life, not being able to talk on the telephone. But there are worse alternatives."

A relative of a deceased alumna responded eloquently. A mother wrote, "Barbara was 43 when she died of cancer. She put her husband through college; maybe this was one of the reasons that her life always seemed highly stressed."

Miscellaneous Results

The vast majority of the respondents perceived that they were financially better off than their parents were at a similar age. A poignant comment from one woman was that she was doing the same financially as her parents, but the difference was that she had only three children while her mother had eight.

The level of parental education reported by each of the respondents was that more fathers, 46%, had graduated from college than mothers, 31%.

This correlates with increased educational opportunities for women, and the fact that many mothers of the baby boomers left college prior to graduation to marry and bear children (Horowitz-Lefkowitz, 1984).

Despite the many political perspectives, 88% of the women in the study said that they would vote for a woman for president if she were nominated and qualified for the job. When these results from the demographic survey were compared to the General Social Survey (GSS) (1987) data for the years 1986 and 1987, similarities were found. An overwhelming majority of the respondents to the national survey replied that they too would vote for a woman for president if she were qualified. In 1985, 83% said that they would vote for a woman, and in 1986, 76% replied in the affirmative. The national sample consisted of 688 males and 846 females in 1985; in 1986, there were 621 males and 849 females. The respondents were ages 18 to 89. The national survey is a modified probability sample. Quotas based on age, sex, and employment status were created to assure the cross-sectional integrity of the sample.

A comparison of political orientation in this study to political orientation in the General Social Survey (1987) is given below.

Question: What are your views on political matters?

| | Frequencies and Percentages | |
	GSS	This Study
a. extremely liberal	31 (2%)	19 (2%)
b. liberal	175 (12%)	135 (14%)
c. slightly liberal	190 (13%)	125 (13%)
d. middle-of-the-road	537 (37%)	144 (15%)
e. slightly conservative	235 (16%)	221 (23%)
f. conservative	178 (12%)	270 (28%)
g. extremely conservative	32 (2%)	19 (2%)
h. not sure	59 (4%)	19 (2%)
i. refused to answer	29 (2%)	10 (1%)
Total Answering	1466	962

However, there are many similarities noted. The sample in this study reflects a more conservative orientation expressing higher percentages in the slightly conservative and conservative categories, except perhaps for the woman who commented that she "had no political opinions before she was 40."

It has been shown that the following variables constitute similarities among the various age groups of midlife women: household income, parental encouragement to seek employment, participation in volunteer activities, participation in regular exercise, and marital status. Differences have been noted among the age groups with respect to variables such as reasons for not being currently employed, living together before marriage, number of times divorced and remarried, number of children, family assistance with children, employment while child-rearing, empty nest following child-rearing, views on political orientation, and change in political views with age. Some of the variables have been enhanced by the personal comments shared by the respondents. The greatest surprise in the results was that age was not significant in determining life satisfaction or anxiety levels. The age factor proved to be similar across all of the age groups.

Conclusions

The hypothesis that the baby-boom cohort would be the least satisfied and the most anxious was disproved in this study. The things that made the midlife women in the study most happy were job status, enjoying one's job, marriage, the presence of children, and good general health. The baby-boom women in this study have remained similar to their older cohorts in many areas. Somewhere during the societal changes, the younger cohorts have maintained many of their traditional values with a few accommodations.

Trends are also evident that indicate that the vast majority of women are choosing to marry and to bear children. The difference appears to be that marriage and childbearing are occurring later in life, and women are having fewer children. The above trends were also replicated in the report on the study of the Vietnam generation (*Enduring Legacies*, 1987). Despite societal changes, societal values appear to be the most preferred options for women in this study.

Furthermore, women who reported that they were married or living with someone demonstrated lower levels of anxiety and higher life satisfaction. Living with someone, rather than committing to marriage, is a social change consistent with increased sexual freedom.

Women who were divorced or never married exhibited lower life satisfaction and higher levels of anxiety. This finding may be contrary to the popular notion that divorced women have been liberated from unhappy marriages and are receiving greater social support than ever before. They are considered to be more self-sufficient, because they have a higher level of education and are self-supporting (Maxwell, 1988). However, the reality is that single parenting and low income are often a reality when women divorce, as noted previously in this chapter by one of the participants in the study.

Employment is an evolving trend, especially for the 80% of the baby-boom women in this study. Even in the older age groups, the majority of the women worked, at least part-time, outside the home. In most instances work was enjoyed and contributed positively to overall life satisfaction. These data correlate with many other studies (*Enduring Legacies*, 1987).

Implications

This study continues to replicate contemporary literature that disproves the belief that midlife women are highly anxious and dissatisfied with their lives. Age did not appear to be a factor in determining anxiety levels and life satisfaction, as all age groups reported virtually the same levels.

In regard to employment, the respondents in this study reported more diversity than ever before. However, the number of women in non-traditional jobs was not significant in this study. It was shown that the trend toward these types of professions was increasing. Although women are currently enjoying status in larger numbers than ever before in the formerly male businesses of engineering and medicine, there is still a dearth, for example, of female engineers and engineering students. Perhaps this will continue to change with a raised consciousness on how women are educated, and the expectations that society places on them.

It is suggested that socialization is responsible for most of the differences between the groups of midlife women in this study. A new form of traditionalism is evident in the baby-boom women who appear to be adopting more conservative lifestyles as they mature. They are searching to make their impact as they head toward becoming the pillars of society. In the aggregate, the baby-boom women are doing it all. They are working to realize their potential and self-imposed expectations. Age and maturity are the emerging factors that lead to conforming to the structural norms that society imposes. Developmental trends will have to be determined through additional studies on this very pivotal life transition. Here is a final quote from one of the women in the study: *"Some run for glory, some run for medals, but I want to run for eternal youth. I want to live long and die young."*

References

Adams, J., Hayes, J., & Hopson, B. (1977). *Transitions*. New York: Universe Books.

Birren, J.E., Kinney, D.K., Shaie, K.W., & Woodruff, D.S. (1981). *Developmental psychology*. Boston: Houghton Mifflin.

Cattell, R.B. (1966). Patterns of change: Measurements in relation to state dimension, trait change, liability, and process concepts. *Handbook of Multivariate Psychology*. Chicago: Rand McNally.

Chodorow, N. (1978). *The reproduction of mothering*. Berkeley: University of California Press.

Crunch Statistical Package. (1987). Oakland, CA: Crunch Software Corporation.

Davis, R.H. (1981). *Aging: Prospects and issues*. Los Angeles: University of Southern California Press.

Duffy, M.E. (1985). A critique of research: A feminine perspective. *Health Care for Women International*, 4(5,6), 341–352.

Ehrenreich, B. (1983). *The hearts of men*. Garden City, NY: Anchor Books.

Enduring legacies: Expressions from the hearts and minds of the Vietnam generation. (1987). Washington, D.C.: Center for New Leadership.

Erikson, E.H. (1950). *Childhood and society*. New York: W.W. Norton.

Friedan, B. (1963). *The feminine mystique*. New York: Dell Publishing Co., Inc.

Friedan, B. (1981). *The second stage*. New York: Summit Books.

General Social Survey. (1972–1987). *Cumulative code book*. Chicago: National Opinion Research Center, University of Chicago.

Gilligan, C. (1982). *In a different voice*. Cambridge, MA: The Harvard University Press.

Gould, R.L. (1978). *Transitions*. New York: Simon & Schuster.

Gribbon, R.T. (1981). *30 year olds and the church: Ministry with the "Baby Boom" generation*. Washington, D.C.: Alban Institute.

Horowitz-Lefkowitz, H. (1984). *Alma mater*. Boston: Beacon Press.

Jones, L.Y. (1981). *Great expectations*. New York: Ballantine Books.

Jung, C.G. (1961). *Memories, dreams, reflections*. New York: Random House.

Keohane, N.O., Rosaldo, M.Z., & Gelpi, B.C. (1981). *Feminist theory*. Chicago: University of Chicago Press.

Kessler-Harris, A. (1982). *Out to work*. New York: Oxford University Press.

Krantzler, M. (1981). *Creative marriage*. New York: Human Science Press.

Krueger, D.H. (1984). *Success and the fear of success in women*. New York: The Free Press.

Lewin, J., & Spates, J. (1970). Hippie values: An analysis of the underground press. *Youth and Society*, 2, 59–72.

Maxwell, E.K. (1988). Status differences in cohorts of aging women. *Health Care for Women International*, 9, 83–91.

McKinlay, J., & McKinlay, S. (1986). *Women and their health in Massachusetts*. Cambridge, MA: Cambridge Research Center.

Miller, W.E. (1982). *American national election study*. Ann Arbor, MI: Center for Political Studies, University of Michigan.

Naisbitt, J. (1982). *Megatrends*. New York: Warner Books.

Neugarten, B. L. (1968). *Middle age and aging*. Chicago: University of Chicago Press.

Neugarten, B.L., Havighurst, R.J., & Tobin, S.S. (1961). The measurement of life satisfaction. *Journal of Gerontology, 16*, 134–143.

Rubin, L.B. (1979). *Women of a certain age*. New York: Harper & Row.

Salamon, M.J., & Conte, V.A. (1984). *Salamon-Conte life satisfaction in the elderly scale*. Odessa, FL: Psychological Assessment Resources, Inc.

Schwartz, F.N. (1989). Management women and the new facts of life. *Harvard Business Review, 1*, 65–76.

Selye, H. (1955). Stress and disease. *Science*. Washington, D.C.: American Association for the Advancement of Science.

Sheehy, G. (1976). *Passages*. New York: Bantam Books.

Silverstone, B., & Hyman, H.K. (1982). *You and your aging parent*. New York: Pantheon Books.

Spielberger, C.D., Gorsuch, R.L., & Luchene, R.E. (1983). *State-trait anxiety inventory*. Palo Alto, CA: Consulting Psychologists Press.

Statistical Abstract of the United States (1985). Washington, D.C.: U.S. Department of Commerce, Bureau of the Census.

"The new baby bloom." (1982, February 22). *Time Magazine*, 52–59.

Wheeler, A.P., Lee, E.S., & Hardy, D.L. (1983). Employment, sense of well-being, and the use of professional services among women. *American Journal of Public Health, 83*(8), 908–911.

White, A.H. (1986). *The charitable behavior of Americans: Management summary*. Commissioned by the Rockefeller Brothers Fund. New York: Yanklovitch, Skelly, & White, Inc.

Chapter 5

Trends and Projections for the Future

The material previously presented has yielded the discussion for the final chapter in this book. The baby-boom generation of midlife women is making its mark on societal norms. I will summarize some of the evolutionary changes here. New social and biological norms are slowly emerging, and there are many predictions of what women will be like in the next century (Aburdene & Naisbitt, 1992; Kegan, 1994; Branscomb, 1994). Some of these predictions are generated through simple deduction, while other authors project creative new insights for the future. The discussion will be divided into sections on emerging theoretical perspectives, health and policy issues, social issues, work patterns for midlife women, and, finally, predictions for the future.

New Theoretical Perspectives

Kegan (1994) presents a complex set of tasks and expectations placed on us by modern life in which the self is constantly learning. He warns that we are being bombarded with multiple outside stimuli and that the information highway that we are creating is only adding to the confusion. Just consider for a moment the intrusion on our solitude, and the competition for our attention from fax machines, answering machines, e-mail, and cellular phones. Our lives have become overwhelmed. The author notes that so many enormous databases have been developed that do not coordinate with each other, leaving us with conflicting allegiances and complete disregard for who we are and the multiple overwhelming roles that we must develop. A new way of looking at human development and transition is essential for looking at individuals' changing roles and dimensions. Kegan emphasizes that we must recognize that the old theories often do not fit our complex and contemporary lives. Taken into consideration are the emotional, cognitive, interpersonal, and intrapersonal experiences of adult development. Diversity and personality are central themes of how an individual progresses.

113

Five levels of consciousness are identified by Kegan (1994), and each presents both tasks and transitions. Level One is the earliest level, representing infancy and childhood. In this level, the individual is egocentric and operates on a moment to moment basis. Level Two includes the process of socialization, in which developmental tasks such as learning to take care of oneself, becoming organized, thinking of others besides oneself, and becoming a good citizen are learned. This stage, as you might imagine, encompasses adolescence. Level Three centers around meeting the demands of parenting and partnering. In the process, one must teach the concepts of power, authority, and control. The traditional community supports this family-centered stage, as well as the caring for the next generation. However, one has the feeling that this level does not take into consideration the unattached, who choose not to parent except in a broad sense. Level Four encompasses looking at others' points of view, another dimension of adult development. Kegan says that this stage is not automatic, uninterrupted, or seamless. It is an evolutionary stage that causes one to question feelings. It is a stage in which the context of self-evaluating and self-governing permits us to take responsibility for our actions in the context of others. In this stage, a new level of personal authority, self-possession, and critical thinking are developed. Finally, Level Five is concerned with the development of mental complexity that includes connecting with our multiple selves, and acquiring a sense of relationships and connectedness. This stage is synonymous with longevity and the wisdom that comes with age and experience. This allows one to step away from oneself and comprehend several views at once. Mediators, who are objective and have the capacity to disassociate from their own point of view, are examples of individuals who have accomplished the tasks set forth in this stage.

Although Kegan draws on previous theorists, he accounts for a postmodernism that also allows for diversity in culture and gender. He brings the study of adult development to another level consistent with changing social norms. He sets no distinct parameters for the tasks described in the adult stages. It is expected that this and other frameworks will address the variance between the baby-boom generation and those who preceded them through the exploration of Kegan's levels of consciousness.

Transitions

Schumacker and Meleis (1994) present the importance of recognizing transition as a central concept in the nursing profession and all of the biological, psychological, and social facets of the human experience. From the literature they have identified, central themes must be considered so that nursing therapeutics can be promotive, preventive, and interventive. Transition may be developmental, situational, and organizational in the context of external transition from health to illness. The midlife transition may encompass all of these. Universal properties of transition are identified as the processes of change in identity, roles and relationships, abilities, patterns of behavior, structure, function, and dynamics. Indicators of healthy transition are self-declaration of well-being, mastery of new roles, and the well-being of relationships.

The authors project that the study of successful transition will be a major theme for research and practice in the future. Certainly, more information surrounding the pivotal midlife transition is sorely needed so that we can create grounded theories on successful aging and coping within the context of evolving societal norms. The authors have provided an essential framework for future application to the mysteries of transition as a central concept.

AIDS and Midlife Women

There is limited research in women and human immunodeficiency virus (HIV), or acquired immune deficiency syndrome (AIDS). In the early days of the AIDS epidemic, researchers did not consider gender, and left women out of the investigations surrounding the disease. At a recent series on women's health and AIDS, Hortensia de los Angeles Amaro, from the Boston University School of Public Health, and an advisor to the U.S. Surgeon General (May, 1994), reported that "women don't get AIDS, they just die from it." Women are getting AIDS more rapidly than men: they had a 15% higher rate in 1990, compared to a 3% rise for males during the same period. There were 293,000 individuals of both sexes infected in 1993, and it is projected that 11.4 million individuals are at risk for contracting AIDS. It is imperative to note that heterosexual contact accounted for 40% of AIDS cases in 1992. This is seen as an emerging trend. Although the incidence in midlife women is small in comparison to younger women, it appears to be only a matter of time before the incidence spreads to this population of women as well.

Hortensia de los Angeles Amaro (May, 1994) suggests that sex, love, and drugs are intertwined in the epidemic in which women allow male partners to undermine safe sex practices because of cultural mores. She uses psychosocial models, such as the Health Belief Model and Self Efficacy Theory (Stretcher, Devellis, Becker, & Rosenstock, 1986), to describe the process through which AIDS is contracted. However, she conjectures that the models do not fit within the parameters of the Hispanic woman's experience. It is implied in the models that an individual has control over her own actions. This may not be evident in a woman's relationship in which a dominant male partner may refuse to wear a condom, or may threaten to leave her if she does not comply.

In some Hispanic cultures, pregnancy validates manhood, and men who may be infected with AIDS are unwilling to use any mechanical methods available to prevent pregnancy. This increases the chances the mother and the unborn fetus have of contracting AIDS or other sexually transmitted disease. The MOMS project, funded by the National Institute on Drug Abuse, in which de los Angeles Amaro is the principal investigator, is seeking answers to solve the dilemma of this dangerous behavior. Through this project, she seeks to change behavior and provide a rationale for the seemingly endless spread of the AIDS virus. The project will facilitate women in gaining self-esteem and offer support to protect the women and their children. A central issue will be exploring the fears that women have of being abused or disconnected because of the conflicts surrounding safe sex. Concerted efforts will be undertaken to involve male partners in safe sex educational programs. This is a deadly issue, and one that will continue to escalate well into the next century. In the end, it will no doubt affect midlife women of all cultures and races in the future.

Women's perceptions about contracting AIDS were investigated by Jesson, Luck, and Taylor (1994). The women in their study were employed in sauna or massage parlors. These women concluded that because they were in a sex industry, it was easier to talk to their clients about condom use. As a result, they remained relatively safe from contracting the disease. The main conclusion is that casual sex may be more dangerous for women. Women who use prevention in their daily lives are thought to be more protected. The implications are that being comfortable with the topic of safe sex may save lives, and educational programs for women about AIDS are essential.

Information

Branscomb (1994) sets forth an interesting premise that impinges on all of our lives. It concerns information management and the projection that we are entering an era of information highways. She has explored implications of the reliability of statistical data and how that information itself is disseminated. She questions the issue of confidentiality, especially as related to the collection of medical information, and more specifically, around the worldwide AIDS epidemic. Most infected individuals would rather not have their confidentiality breached for fear of repercussions if their illness is revealed. This presents an emerging predicament. One may also question the validity of information that is somehow collected when all of the information about a specific disease is not forthcoming. As in the case of AIDS, medical professionals are reluctant to divulge confidences. This is dramatically illustrated by Branscomb in the discrepancies she found between the World Health Organization's estimate of 40 million cases of AIDS worldwide by the year 2000, and the estimate of 110 million cases predicted by a consortium of independent health care professionals. We can only imagine the quandary this presents for health care policy makers. How will it be possible to foresee future estimates to provide sufficient resources to deal with the epidemic as it proliferates around the world? Branscomb recounts that, in the past, public health officials have tracked infectious diseases by identifying infected persons. This method has served us well in the past. Other sexually transmitted diseases, for example, were treated, tracked, and contacts identified to prevent further spread of the infection. We should not discount the fact that several devastating diseases such as smallpox and polio have been eradicated worldwide through both this type of surveillance and, of course, vaccination.

Today there are numerous technological resources to instantly track individuals and their contacts when an outbreak occurs. We are hindered, however, by a myriad of legal implications. Also consider the problem of obtaining medical insurance when an individual's medical records reveal a chronic illness or HIV infection. Branscomb advises that these databases, so urgent in the eradication of disease, may be elusive until we can first trust the integrity of a medical information system, and all citizens of the United States are covered with universal medical insurance allowing universal treatment.

Projecting the Future of Breast Cancer

A very promising new development was reported by researchers at the University of Southern California Norris Cancer Center, where clinical trials on a new therapeutic vaccine for treating breast cancer are under way (Trojan Family, Winter, 1994). Phase one of the study, in Canada, indicated a significant reduction in the size of breast tumors. Phase two involves 42 women with early stage breast cancer metastases. If successful, the research could provide women with alternative treatment modalities such as surgery, radiation, and chemotherapy, claims Principal Investigator, Malcolm Mitchell. The vaccine stimulates the body's depressed immune system against a sugar that surrounds the cancer cells. The process is called Active Specific Immunotherapy. A similar substance is also being developed to treat melanoma, the deadly skin cancer. With trials such as these, we are encouraged that breast cancer may be successfully treated. It is the hope of all women that the cause of breast cancer will be identified in the near future so that we may know exactly what kind of preventative measures can be undertaken.

In a report from the 1994, 160th meeting of the National Meeting of the American Association for the Advancement of Science (AAAS), many of the leading speakers were well-known researchers in the breast cancer field (Reyes, 1994). Notably, Dr. Graham Colditz of the Harvard Nurses Health Study and Dr. Elihu Richter from Israel gave some revealing testimony about breast cancer.

Colditz concluded from his longitudinal study, cited in Chapter 3, that short-term use of estrogens for treatment of menopausal symptoms did not appear to be harmful. When estrogens were continued in women ages 60 and older, however, a marked increase in breast cancer incidence was noted. The addition of progesterone did not offer any protection. With regard to the osteoporosis connection, Colditz reported that heart disease and osteoporosis are most severe in women in their 80s and any protection from estrogen replacement is lost after 4 years. According to Reyes (1994), Colditz points out that exercise and vitamin E are possible deterrents to heart disease and osteoporosis, but this is not definitive. In a study that I have recently conducted, the preliminary results indicate that of the 1,000 women in the sample, roughly ⅔ do not take vitamins regularly. Of the 65 women who reported having breast cancer the results were similar. Only 23 of the breast cancer victims reported taking vitamin E, 18 reported vitamin D, 27 vitamin C, and 21 took vitamin B daily while the remainder did not. However, 31 of the women with cancer did report taking a multivitamin every day (Jacobson, 1994). This is certainly an area for future research.

The Israeli connection was another interesting facet of Reyes report (1994). It has to do with the premise of the medical community knowing the cause of breast cancer but doing nothing because of the political and economic implications. Dr. Elihu Richter is renowned for his report on the sensational drop in the incidence of breast cancer in Israel between 1976 and 1986. Richter described the ban on organochlorines such as DDT and its by-products because of the high levels of these substances found in Israeli milk products. The most damning evidence of insecticide infestation was the report of the levels of benzene hexachloride found in the breast milk of Israeli women. It was at a level 800 times higher than that found in the breast milk of American women. When these substances were banned, there was a dramatic drop in the rates of breast cancer morbidity and mortality in Israeli women.

Reyes (1994) reported that Richter was critical of both the American Cancer Society and the National Cancer Institute for failing to support methods of primary prevention. Rather, they have been focusing on methods of treatment that have done little to reduce breast cancer incidence in the past 25 years in the United States. A concerted public policy is needed to reduce environmental hazards, and empirical data must be collected to validate this intervention.

Social Issues

Lesbian Relationships and Lifestyles

I have left this discussion for now because it has only been since the late 1970s and early 1980s that any validated, empirical data were presented on the lesbian experience, making the study of lesbian behavior a recent and emerging trend. Prior to this period, lesbians were described by the medical profession as sick, dangerous, aggressive, tragically unhappy, deceitful, contagious, and self-destructive. They were often treated by psychiatrists with electric shock, confinement, psychosurgery, hormonal injections, and psychotropic drugs. Lesbianism was treated as a hidden condition stemming from homophobia and ignorance about homosexuality. Successful treatment, it was believed earlier, was to change the homosexuality to heterosexuality (Gentry, 1992).

Lesbians were condemned and maltreated by medical professionals. This resulted in lesbian women avoiding the medical system altogether for fear of humiliation, or worse still, hazardous procedures (Stevens, 1992). Stevens conducted a 20-year review of the literature on lesbians, much of which was unavailable from the lay or government press. She found that there are deeply ingrained prejudices among members of the health care delivery system. As a consequence, lesbians have avoided medical care. This presents a serious lack in the system. Stevens claims that it is only through sensitivity and education of health care professionals that the problem can be remedied. Most of the women in the research studies were white, middle class, well-educated, and many of them had health insurance. As a result of the consistent negative treatment, lesbians often sought health care "out of the mainstream" in alternative medical clinics. Poor, uninsured, lesbian women of color were described as having to deal with not only racial discrimination, but also the prejudice attributed to same-sex orientation by medical caregivers.

Trippet and Bain (1992) also report that lesbians are isolated from society and tend to hide their orientation in order to avoid intolerance and hostile attitudes directed toward them. In their study, lesbians implied that they preferred nurse practitioner managed clinics in which the providers were women who were sensitive to their needs.

Robertson (1992) states that lesbians are an invisible minority in the health care delivery system, although they are estimated to make up 10%

of the female population. It has been only recently that increasing numbers of gay and lesbian individuals have "come out" to openly express their sexual preferences. Robertson also found that most physicians assume that their patients are heterosexual and are usually negative when confronted by a lesbian who identifies herself. There is often disregard for the feelings of partners as well as issues of confidentiality. She concludes that nurses, in particular, have the opportunity to provide safe, sensitive, and preventative health care to lesbians as should all health care professionals.

In 1973, the American Psychiatric Association declassified homosexuality as a mental illness. Most believe that this was the watershed event that is slowly leading to the end of prejudice by mental health professionals and others (Gentry, 1992). However, not until society examines its collective beliefs about the homosexual lifestyle will the nonjudgmental, effective care be delivered that the gay community has the right to expect. Gentry, in describing other characteristics of the lesbian community, also cites that the Centers for Disease Control (1990) recounted that lesbians are at very low risk for developing HIV infection and other forms of sexually transmitted diseases.

It was found that the majority of lesbians desire to have children and to parent (Gentry, 1992). This is often accomplished by artificial insemination through sperm banks. However, there is an enormous amount of backlash in the heterosexual community regarding lesbian parenting. As a result, it is almost impossible for lesbians to adopt a child through normal channels. The choice of selecting either artificial insemination or heterosexual intercourse is of utmost importance. Potentially, the lesbian woman may be faced with custody battles later on if the sperm donor is known, or the father who impregnated the woman claims custody.

In a study of midlife lesbians, Kirkpatrick (1989) found that 25–30% had been married at some point in their lives and at least half had children. A familiar pattern occurs when the women raise their families and, after 20 or 30 years of marriage, leave their husbands for a relationship with another woman. Relationships with adolescent children often become strained because of peer pressure, and fear of embarrassment because of their mother's sexual orientation. This can be most heartwrenching for the lesbian mother who is trying to cope with numerous stressors that surround her own identity and the midlife transition.

Nevertheless, lesbians tend to have large social networks of friends who may ease the loneliness and discord. Current theories of adult development do not account for these variances. Kirkpatrick (1989) reports that the search for intimacy is a central theme in the older lesbian's life, although it may become overwhelming for a lesbian couple when privacy in the relationship becomes an issue. Most lesbians are reported to be committed to their partners and plan for a long life together. The fear of grow-ing old is not generally emphasized by lesbians as it is by the heterosexual community. This is seen as a positive aspect of the lesbian experience. Kirk-patrick stresses that midlife lesbians may find the life satisfaction and support that is often lacking in the heterosexual community. Perhaps, through education and further research, this emerging societal trend will become more accepted. Then the lesbian community will be able to live without fear and hostility in a nonjudgmental society.

Homelessness

This is presented as an emerging concern for women and children that has become an urgent social issue. Stone (1989) has connected homeless-ness with the feminization of poverty. This is a result, she states, of pater-nalistic laws and customs that encouraged female dependency on men. She cites the tradition of British common law that has served as the key-stone of American law and policy. This implies that a married couple is viewed as a single person, with the husband accepting responsibility for all the legal and economic matters. These policies, Stone claims, have left many women one man away from poverty.

Stone (1989) concedes that many women in our society work out-side the home and are earning a pay for work. Their work histories, how-ever, often reveal patterns of midlife career entry, intermittent employ-ment, and frequent job changes. The result is that these women are not vested in retirement plans, nor are they prepared to support themselves in the possible occurrence of widowhood or divorce. In addition, women in midlife are called upon to care for elderly parents at a time when their children have left home, and they might have availed themselves of work outside the home. Women are generally the assigned caregivers in our society and return to the work force may be interrupted by family de-mands. Even when women have sufficient work time to be vested in pen-sion plans, their plans yield substantially lower amounts than male pri-vate pension plans. Perhaps, in the future, the baby-boom generation of midlife women will not be faced with this dilemma because of its longer, uninterrupted work history. This may not be plausible, however, if the predictions of the Commonwealth Fund Commission report on Elderly People Living Alone (1987) become a reality. In the report, male poverty by the year 2020 is expected to diminish substantially, while there will be no change in female rates. A part of this rate is attributed to the de-mographic situation in which women outlive men. Stone (1989) suggests, however, that the gender gap in employment patterns is the real expla-nation. Baby-boom generation women, as previously inferred, are in a position to reverse the feminization of poverty. It is essential that contemporary women realize the numerous strategies that are available for them to begin early in life to prepare themselves so they will not be faced with poverty or homelessness.

Montgomery (1994), through her research, indicates that homelessness, especially in women and children, has become an urgent concern. She alleges that the causes of homelessness are varied, but attributes them to changing economic conditions and cuts in federal spending for affordable housing. There is an emerging face of homelessness in which women and children are replacing the stereotypic profile of older, alcoholic men. Not only are many of the women faced with poverty, but many are fleeing from violent and abusive homes. Several nursing studies have been undertaken to explore the intricacies related to homeless women. In these studies, there are indications that homeless women attempt to cope with their situations through supportive relationships. Homelessness is depicted as a severe loss that often calls on spiritual mechanisms to overcome the pain. This can be a positive dimension in discovery of personal strengths and the subsequent coping to make a new life in a home of one's own.

In her study of 7 women between 33 and 53 years old, Montgomery illustrates the characteristics of previously homeless women. Most of these women grew up in dysfunctional homes, and 6 of the 7 participants had been sexually or physically abused as children. When these women became homeless, it was viewed by them as temporary, and was the result of attempting to break away from abusive and oppressive situations. They were willing to endure the temporary disruption of homelessness in order to create meaningful and self-actualized lives for themselves and their children. They left home because they had finally hit rock bottom in lives filled with drugs or as victims of family violence. Personal strengths such as stubborn pride, positive orientation and hope, moral structure with a keen sense of right and wrong, and clarity of focus with stoic determination gave them the strength to try for a better life away from the abuse and disruption. In finding connections and sustaining relationships, these women were able to overcome self-doubt and make a new beginning. Community support was essential in providing shelter, recovery interventions, training, and educational programs. Because of the kindness and generosity extended to them, when the women recovered, they expressed a strong commitment to give back and help others who were undergoing the same fight for survival. Some even became counselors. A key element in the recovery process, attained through counseling and support, was a lack of bitterness related to their painful prior lives.

Montgomery's study (1994) is an enlightening account that reveals the strengths of these women. She warns, nevertheless, that post-trauma stress is often still present as these women simultaneously cope with new stressors in their current lives. Additional research and community support of programs for homeless women are emerging and necessary to prevent despair and continued disruption.

Family Violence

The question of family violence and violence against women is put before us every day as we read the daily newspapers and watch the news on television. Is this a contemporary phenomenon? Is our society so violent that we have become numbed to its seriousness? Is there an increase in violence, or is it just reported more often and exploited by sensational journalists? Whatever the answer, it is important to note that the damage to a woman's self-esteem when she is battered by someone she knows, loves, and trusts is devastating.

A woman is battered every 13 seconds in the United States, and every day at least 4 are slain by their batterers (Aburdene & Naisbitt, 1992). There may be over 4 million women battered each year. Harrington and Estes (1994) report that the major reason for women seeking emergency room treatment is for injuries sustained through a battering. They contend that a concerted effort must be undertaken to change this depraved behavior. Research about why women accept this treatment must be conducted and we must also discover the precursors of violent behavior in men. Laws must be enacted in all states that really protect women from being stalked and murdered by a revengeful, jealous lover or husband. Women must be supported by community services and protected by the court system. Conceivably, a change in societal values will have to be undertaken through rigorous educational programs that sensitize abusive men against violence and teach respect for women and their children.

Aburdene and Naisbitt (1992) declare that 25% of all women will be victims of violence at some point in their lives. This is a shocking prediction. The authors offer five areas in which solutions empower women victims to survive the battering. They are: legislation and tough enforcement, self-defense for women, more women in law enforcement, and dramatizations to sensitize everyone from school children to professionals about the effects of violence. Finally, they suggest attracting more males into the antiviolence movement so that they will be educated to act as role models for other men.

Since the medical profession, through emergency room service, is often the initial contact for a battered woman, The Council on Scientific Affairs of the American Medical Association (1992) has set forth recommendations to deal with the problem. In the past, the medical and law enforcement communities have been somewhat unresponsive in dealing with women who were victims of violence, making this response most encouraging. Embodied in these recommendations is alerting the health care community to the seriousness of the problem so that it can meet the needs of the victims. Regular screening of women who may be victims, validation and sensitivity to the victimization experienced by the women, accurate recording of the trauma and appropriate referrals, inclusion of training programs for medical education, and, finally, development of treatment protocols are all proposed as interim solutions to the problem (Council Reports, 1992). This hopeful sign indicates that the medical profession and society at large are finally addressing the problem, seeking answers, and beginning to employ preventative measures. Activists against violence and increasing numbers of women entering into elected political office may finally put an end to this terrible societal aberration.

A Critique of Feminism

Sommers (1994) presents a critique of what she claims is the inaccurate information that is being circulated about violence perpetrated on women. She gives an example of a totally inaccurate story, attributed to The March of Dimes, that was carried in the national media. A bogus account is discussed in which large numbers of birth defects were reported to be the result of pregnant women being battered. When Sommers traced the story to its roots, she found that it had arisen from an embellishment of research presentation in which there was a comparison between screening for birth defects and screening pregnant women for battering. The story was finally retracted when The March of Dimes reported that they had never seen any research on the subject, in spite of the fact that journalists around the country were reporting the story.

The author goes on to say that American feminists are controlled by women who are spreading false information about a dominating male patriarchy that is dictating to women in this country. Because of this, men are violent toward women. She uses an example of egregious information put out by a coalition of women's groups warning women that on Super Bowl Sunday, in 1993, 40% more women would be battered than on any other day of the year. This sensational figure was carried in newspapers all over the country. In the process, women were warned to get out of the house during the game. When one reporter traced the source of the 40% figures, they were based on the conjecture of a women's group who had misinterpreted the study that reported just the opposite of what was printed in the national media. Again, the story was finally retracted by the media. When shelters and emergency rooms were actually monitored on Super Bowl Sunday, no deviation from the norm was found.

Sommers (1994) continues that rather than women losing ground, in the 1980s and now the 1990s, they have become more successful than ever before in attaining success in the public sector. Regarding the wage gap between salaries for women and men, Sommers reports that the 1992 figures for parity are that college-educated women received 73¢ on the dollar of what college-educated men earned. This is the highest rate ever. Reasons given for the still existing discrepancy is not discrimination, but rather she suggests because women are reported to work fewer hours per week than men. Other rationale given for the disparity are shorter length of experience and interruption in work to bear and rear children. In addition, the author states that women are less likely to work long hours and weekends than are men. However, when the earnings of childless females are analyzed their wages rose to within 10% of male wages. Possibly, she has compromised her argument when she admits that there may still be unequal household responsibilities between men and women, and that business is not culpable in this instance.

At any rate, Sommers does remind us that sensational journalism must be questioned and sources verified before judgments are made. She is right in claiming that women are slowly achieving equity, but these gains have mainly come about after years of struggle and protest. One must reflect on the fact that women were only given the right to vote in America in 1920, and colleges for women were not established until the mid-1800s.

Health Care Policy for Women

In the past, the health care establishment has considered women's health mainly as a reproductive and gynecological issue. It is obvious that the present system does not provide a holistic perspective, nor does it consider other aspects of a woman's physical, emotional, and social needs. In 1990, The Society for the Advancement for Women's Health was established to put forth an agenda on women's health. It established a comprehensive overview of the health and psychological issues that are specific to women, in addition to the reproductive issues. Harrington and Estes (1994) describe this society whose purpose it is to disseminate information and consult with women who are leaders in the community and the health care field, and who are consumers of their own health care.

Women's health courses are slowly emerging in nursing education programs for advanced practice nurses. However, it is true that nursing education has been highly focused on reproductive issues, acute care, and long-term care for the elderly. Further, there is no primary health medical specialty specifically devoted to the practice of women's health beyond reproduction and gynecological care. Most women need to see several health care professionals in order to receive any type of comprehensive care (Harrington & Estes, 1994). In the present system a woman must be assertive in expressing her health care needs. Otherwise, they may be over-looked, or misunderstood because a particular care giver has inadequate knowledge about a particular aspect of women's health. It is also recog-nized that research on women's health, specifically cardiovascular disease, must be accelerated. It is expected that advocacy groups, like the one mentioned above, and others, like the National Women's Health Network, will finally put the issue of comprehensive women's health in the forefront of health care policy.

Harrington and Estes' (1994) report on the Society for the Advance-ment of Women's Health Research Agenda echoes others' concerns. The agenda report counsels that before any medical regimen is implemented addressing women's health, it is imperative to include "interactions be-tween the biological, psychological, and social issues that impact women" (p. 385). Furthermore, a macro version of factors that will eventually lead to improvement in health care policies for women is presented. It begins with women assuming leadership roles in academe, especially in the medical profession. It is admonished that women should not emulate male leadership styles, but rather they should present a feminine bear-ing that demands respect and is true to one's gender. Developing a spe-cialty that deals with women's health in its entirety is also put forth so that women will stop being viewed in terms of their reproductive organs. Nursing education and other health care professions curricula should also continue to respond to the idea of specialization in women's health. Ex-panded access to care for poor and underserved women is of premier importance.

The Women's Health Equity Act of 1991 was a pivotal event guaran-teeing a legislative agenda for women that includes research, preventa-tive measures, and services. Aburdene and Naisbitt (1992) join in the ex-pectation that women's issues will continue to be addressed on the national policy level. Increased funding for additional health care resources and research may be in question. However, in the current climate of cost re-duction and a balanced federal budget, only time will tell.

Education of Women

One would assume with all that we have read about the increased op-portunities of the baby-boom generation that there is finally equity in America's classrooms. The American Association of University Women

(AAUW) (1992) disputes this assumption and claims that gender equality is still lacking. Girls are not receiving the same quality, or quantity, as their brothers in the classroom. The idea that girls are shortchanged may lead to negative consequences in the context of the continued economic stability of our nation. Girls are often diverted from science, mathematics, and technology courses that are essential for their future participation in the work force. Since women make up half of the population, we are at great risk if we do not fix the problem in the very near future. The report will hopefully be a basis for new education policies that will encompass the needs of girls in our society. Some of the observations made in the study are shocking. Girls receive less attention than boys in the classroom, African American students have less interactions with teachers than do Caucasian girls, and sexual harassment of girls by boys is increasing in the nation's schools (p. 2). There are few studies on how girls from low-income and minority groups fare, but the inference is that these groups also receive inadequate education.

Teachers' attitudes and actions reveal a tendency to eliminate girls from answering questions and being spontaneous in the classrooms. Boys are especially favored in math classes. Even when girls excel in the science, math, and technology classes, they are less likely to pursue scientific careers. It is postulated that a loss of self-esteem and confidence is the reason. When tested, the decline in girls' self-esteem and confidence was twice that for boys' as they moved from elementary to high school levels (AAUW, 1992).

When textbooks were analyzed, the contributions of women were left out or trivialized. Health education is deficient, and inclusion of reproduction and sexually transmitted diseases is virtually nonexistent. This may be part of the reason for the proliferation of pregnancy and sexually transmitted diseases among teenagers.

Dropping out of school is also seen as an emerging trend, especially in the Puerto Rican and Cuban American cultures. When surveyed, the reasons given by the girls, other than pregnancy, was likely to be because of family-related problems. Many of these girls were expected to help the family rather than attend school (AAUW, 1992, p. 5).

The implications of this highly publicized report are far-reaching. The gender gap appears to be alive in the education system, where boys are apparently favored over girls. Our nation cannot afford to lose so much of its valuable resource through this oversight. Baby-boom women, many of whom have overcome the educational system, are in a position to support the efforts of the AAUW and advocate for change. The question of same-sex schools is also put forth as an alternative for boys and girls. We can expect an increased awareness of the deficits in the education system and, hopefully, change that will recognize the talents of both boys and girls.

Working Women

In an interesting study of graduates of the Harvard University professional schools, Swiss and Walker (1993) surveyed female graduates who were ten years into their working careers. The graduates came from the schools of business, law, and medicine. In all, 902 women responded yielding a 51% rate of return. Three-quarters of the baby-boom women in the sample were married and two-thirds of them had children under 12. Of these, 89% worked outside the home. Some had blended families with children.

The purpose of the study was to find how working mothers are leading their lives, and whether the glass ceiling or maternal wall were in place. The consensus from these, now professional, baby-boom women was that there was still little progress seen with regard to family considerations in the workplace. Motherhood definitely put careers at risk. Many of these women who purportedly *had it all* speak of feeling conflict in their lives, and many are seeking alternatives. They notice a lack of traditional family lifestyle with everyone in the family working because of the need for dual income. The women in the study who were deemed to be most successful were those who had given up family life to succeed. Adopting *male roles* in the workplace was seen as a survival mechanism. These women reported that they had to work harder to achieve, existed with less sleep, and sacrificed leisure time. The notion of the *mommy tract* was rejected because of its lack of uniformity and the feeling that it removed them from the competition. Motherhood generally equated with not being taken seriously in the workplace.

Despite the implication that men are increasingly sharing in the household responsibilities while their wives work, most of these women rejected that notion. Further, they wondered why the term *working father* was not one that was in common usage. It should be noted, however, that some of the women reported that their spouses were supportive. In spite of this, most reported time spent away from family was generally resented by spouses and children (Swiss & Walker, 1993).

A new model of professional women emerged in the study in which women chose to sequence career and family. These women stayed home for a period of time to parent and then reentered when the children became somewhat independent. In spite of the fact that 85% said that reducing hours to care for family was detrimental to their careers, most did. Many changed jobs to accommodate family needs, but 96% went back to work before their child's first birthday.

There is still another wrinkle in the work and family dilemma for many women who have postponed childbearing. At some point, almost universally, they realize that the biological clock is ticking, and when they decide to attempt pregnancy, they discover fertility problems. Unfortunately, the fertility business has expanded dramatically, trying to meet the needs of baby-boom women.

Many women were left angry and frustrated because of the double message presented by society in which they are encouraged to succeed, but also expected to bear and rear the children with very little societal support. The authors conclude that there are no easy answers. A few optimistic trends have emerged. Women are seeking balanced lives in which they are taken seriously. They must find individual solutions that are comfortable and work toward them because the workplace presently is not user friendly to family life (Swiss & Walker, 1993). In a revealing feature story, the *Wall Street Journal*'s Rochelle Sharpe (March 29, 1994) relates that although women are making strides, men are firmly in the top jobs in many of the businesses in the United States. Thirty years after the Civil Rights Act and the barring of sex discrimination, women have entered the white-collar world. However, they are not matching gains in managerial jobs. Only 30% of the managers in 38,059 companies that were surveyed by the Equal Opportunity Commission in 1992 were women. Furthermore, women make up less than 5% of vice presidential positions in companies. Sharpe claims that it will take another 20 to 30 years for women to reach parity with men. Women in this article also reported that they are not taken seriously. They are often given unimportant jobs that present them with little hope of breaking through the glass ceiling.

According to Sharpe (1994), the women who are slowly rising to the top are seen as adapting to the company culture. One such woman at Ford shares the same singlemindedness about automobiles as her male colleagues. She has even dismantled an engine in her spare bedroom. This same woman lives in a different city than her husband and says that if being in the same house with one's husband is important, then it is a barrier to rising upwards in the corporation. It is obvious that this type of commitment to a job is less ingrained in women than in men in our society.

On the subject of women helping women (*Wall Street Journal*, March 29, 1994), it is reported that career woes cannot be blamed on men entirely. One example is the Turtle Wax Company, chaired by a woman, but with only 11% of its managers female. Some companies, on the other hand, like Wells Fargo and May department stores, have 60 to 66% of their managerial positions filled with women. The least user friendly to employment of women managers are the Nucor Steel Corporation (2.6%) and Ohio Edison (3.3%). One might argue that a steel company does not attract women, but what is the excuse for an electric company?

Women in science do not fare much better than women in business according to a story in *The Boston Globe* (January 17, 1994). Reporting on a National Research Council study, it was found only 12% of engineers and scientists in industry are women. Several factors impinge on these findings. First, women are still not choosing careers in the sciences, as evidenced by the lopsided amount of degrees they are awarded, compared to men, in these fields. When they do choose these professions, there is a male/female gulf in starting salaries between engineers and scientists. Women's starting salaries average $21,000, while males in the same fields average $29,500 to start. Industries also note that women are almost twice more likely to leave their jobs, or choose academic or government work. The issue of the unwillingness of industry to provide for flexibility in dealing with family issues was cited as a major reason for the lack of women in these fields. These issues sum up the seemingly insurmountable hurdles that women face in achieving success in the public sector. Will the next century be magical and remove these obstacles for women? One can only hope that these women may follow, in large numbers, the women who have succeeded in an increasingly humanistic environment.

Predictions

In an anthology of prediction of lifetrends for the millennium, Gerber, Wolff, Klores, and Brown (1989) declare that demographics will determine our fate. The forecast that the baby-boom generation is not likely to enjoy the benefit of social security looms large. The rationale is that the baby-boom generation produced the *baby bust* and have not had enough children to produce a sufficient contributing work force. Although the baby boomers may earn less than their parents, they are destined to inherit the wealth of their affluent parents.

Conversely, the baby-boom generation had to get in line for everything and old age will not be an exception. There will be a means test to get benefits and the rich will not be eligible. Along with these adverse comments, the authors project that the baby bust will be taxed at higher rates than their parents in order to pay for their parents' benefits. The age when one is eligible to receive benefits will, no doubt, be raised as well. However, the baby-boom generation is expected to be healthier and more robust than previous generations, and this may not be such an adverse development as predicted. Immigration will also help to defray some of the burden, but many see this as adding to the problem since many new immigrants are poor and need government support in order to survive.

A positive aspect of the graying of America, with 51 million people over 65 by the year 2020, is that there will be less ageism because such a large percentage of the population will be older. Older workers will be in demand rather than shunned. Because we will age healthier, there will be a crowding of elderly snowbirds vacationing during the winter in warm climates. Competition will be keen for their business, and they will probably be offered senior discounts. Clothing will be designed to be comfortable, not for teenagers with perfect bodies.

These well-educated baby-boom elders are also projected to be more sensitive to family issues. Many have had multiple marriages and are veterans of multi-lifestyle family arrangements. Many have been single parents, and they are all projected to be closer to their children. Divorce situations may necessitate grandparents remaining close to their former in-laws for the purpose of enjoying positive relationships with their grandchildren. Family reunions will replace family dinners because of geographical diversity and large family networks. The situation of elders living great distances from their children may lead to elder care being performed at a distance. It is expected that various forms of living arrangements and managed care will be substituted for elderly baby boomers taking care of their even older parents (Gerber et al., 1989). One wonders if nursing homes and the home health care industries will survive. Who will their clients be with all of these wonderfully healthy, robust baby-boom senior citizens who will be enjoying their golden years in relative good health?

Here are some of my own deductive predictions.

1. The feminist movement as we have known it will be replaced by women reaching the top levels in government and continuing to advocate for women's equity in and out of the home.
2. Increasing numbers of competent women will be found in the board rooms of major corporations.
3. A woman will become president of the United States.
4. A plethora of new family and parenting patterns will emerge as we see older parents with young children. It will be normal to see parents who look like grandparents attending PTA meetings and becoming Girl Scout leaders and sports team coaches.
5. If the current trend toward unmarried teen pregnancies continues, there will be an increase in the numbers of single-parent families who will need to be supported by the community at large.
6. Increased attention will be given to ecological concerns, and the baby-boom generation will be in the vanguard of this movement. Increased awareness about the health implications of toxic waste, insecticides, and overmedicalization are values that this generation has espoused more than any other.
7. The midlife transition will be explored and more fully understood by the baby-boom generation of midlife women than

those women who preceded them. They will make it a positive and exciting life experience as they pave the way for future generations.

I wish them all happiness, good health, and good fortune as they make their way.

References

Aburdene, P., & Naisbitt, J. (1992). *Megatrends for women.* New York: Ballantine Books.

American Association of University Women. (1992). *How schools shortchange girls: Executive summary.* Commissioned by the AAUW Education Foundation and researched by Wellesley College Center for Research on Women.

Branscomb, A.W. (1994). *Who owns information?* New York: Basic Books.

Centers for Disease Control. (1990, June). National AIDS Information Clearing-house. *Female to female transmission of HIV.*

Commonwealth Fund Commission on Elderly People Living Alone. (1987). *Old, alone, and poor: A plan for reducing poverty among elderly people living alone.* New York: The Commonwealth Fund.

Council Reports. (1992). Violence against women. *Journal of the American Medical Association, 267*(23), 3184–3189.

de los Angeles Amaro, H. (1994, May). *Women and AIDS.* Paper presented at a Women's Health Series. Sponsor: The Massachusetts Public Health Association, Boston, MA.

Gentry, S. (1992). Caring for lesbians in a homophobic society. *Health Care for Women International, 13*(2), 173–180.

Gerber, J., Wolff, J., Klores, W., & Brown, G. (1989). *Lifetrends: The future of baby boomers and other aging Americans.* New York: Macmillian Publishing Company.

Harrington, C., & Estes, C.L. (1994). *Health policy and nursing.* Boston: Jones and Bartlett Publishers.

Jacobson, J.M. (1994). *Health behaviors of clients of a suburban mammography center.* Unpublished study.

Jesson, J., Luck, M., & Taylor, J. (1994). Working women in the sex industry and their perception of risk from HIV/AIDS. *Health Care for Women International, 15*(1), 1–9.

Kegan, R. (1994). *In over our heads.* Cambridge, MA: Harvard University Press.

Kirkpatrick, M.D. (1989). Middle age and the lesbian experience. *Women's Studies Quarterly, 17,* 87–96.

Montgomery, C. (1994). Swimming upstream: The strengths of women who survive homelessness. *Advances in Nursing Science, 16*(3), 34–45.

Reyes, L. (May/June, 1994). Yes, there is a known cause of breast cancer. *The Network News: National Women's Health Network, 19*(3), 3–8.

Robertson, M.M. (1992). Lesbians as an invisible minority in the health services arena. *Health Care for Women International, 13*(2), 155–163.

Sanford, L.T., & Donovan, M.E. (1984). *Women and self-esteem.* New York: Penguin Books.

Schumacker, K.L., & Meleis, A.I. (1994). Transitions: A central concept in nursing. *IMAGE: Journal of Scholarship, 26*(2), 119–127.

Sharpe, R. (1994, March 29). Women make strides, but men stay firmly in top company jobs. *The Wall Street Journal,* pp. 1, 10.

Sommers, C.H. (1994). *Who stole feminism?* New York: Simon & Schuster.

Stevens, P.E. (1992). Lesbian health care research: A review of the literature from 1970–1990. *Health Care for Women International, 13*(2), 91–120.

Stone, R.L. (1989). The feminization of poverty among the elderly. *Women's Studies Quarterly, 17,* 20–34.

Stretcher, V.J., Devellis, B.M., Becker, M.H., & Rosenstock, I.M. (1986). The role of self-efficacy in achieving health behavior change. *Health Education Quarterly, 13,* 73–91.

Swiss, D.J., & Walker, J.P. (1993). *Women and the work/family dilemma.* New York: John Wiley & Sons, Inc.

The Boston Globe. (1994, January 17). *Female scientists making few gains,* p. 43.

The Boston Globe. (1994, January 17). *Women in Science.*

The Trojan Family. (Winter, 1994). *New Hope for Women.* Los Angeles: University of Southern California, 13.

The Wall Street Journal. (1994, March 29). *Do women help women?,* p. 10.

Trippet, S.E., & Bain, J. (1992). Reasons American lesbians fail to seek traditional health care. *Health Care for Women International, 13*(2), 145–153.

Index